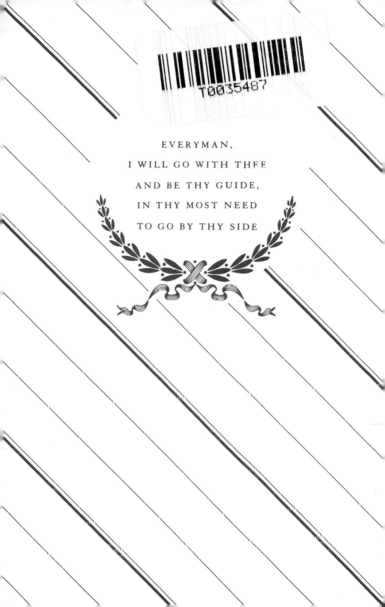

EVERYMAN,
I WILL GO WITH THEE
AND BE THY GUIDE,
IN THY MOST NEED
TO GO BY THY SIDE

SPELLBOUND

POEMS OF MAGIC
AND
ENCHANTMENT

••••••••

EDITED BY
HAROLD SCHECHTER
AND KIMIKO HAHN

EVERYMAN'S LIBRARY
POCKET POETS

Alfred A. Knopf New York London Toronto

THIS IS A BORZOI BOOK
PUBLISHED BY ALFRED A. KNOPF

This selection by Kimiko Hahn and Harold Schechter
first published in Everyman's Library, 2024
Copyright © 2024 by Everyman's Library

A list of acknowledgments to copyright owners appears
at the back of this volume.

everymanslibrary.com

ISBN 978-0-593-53631-5

Typography by Peter B. Willberg

Typeset in the UK by Input Data Services Ltd, Bridgwater, Somerset

Printed and bound in Germany
by GGP Media GmbH, Pössneck

CONTENTS

LIVES OF THE MAGICIANS

SPELLS, CHARMS, INCANTATIONS

FOREWORD

Cultural anthropologists of an earlier era, like the field's founding father E. B. Tylor, regarded magic as an archaic belief system utterly vanquished by modern science. Tylor, however, failed to take into account the persistence of the primitive in the civilized world. While it's true that few of us pursue our goals by occult means, magical thinking is evident in many areas of contemporary life. Shopkeepers frame their first dollar bills as good luck charms. Professional athletes refuse to take the field without lacing their shoes in a ritualistic manner. Wedding guests throw rice to ensure fertility in the newlyweds. Car owners believe that washing their vehicles is a guaranteed way to bring on rain. We may no longer believe that trees are the sacred habitations of deities but many of us still knock on wood, and the most confirmed atheist is likely to say "God bless you" when someone sneezes. As the historian of magic Chris Gosden has observed, while we rationalists may scoff at the notion that we can injure our enemies by sticking pins into their effigies, "most of us would find it very hard to stab a photo of a loved one."

That our modern, technologically advanced Western society is shot through with magic should come as no surprise since, on its deepest levels, the human psyche continues to operate much as it did in pre-historic times. And like other fundamental phenomena that define who and what we are as a species – love and aggression, morality and religion, dream and fantasy – magic, as the selections in this anthology show, has been a central subject of poetry.

There is another link between poetry and magic. Because they often have the sense that their art springs from an arcane source of power – that "they are merely conduits for a force beyond themselves" (in the words of Paul Muldoon) – poets sometimes speak of their creative process as a form of conjuring. The outstanding example is William Butler Yeats, an ardent devotee of the occult arts, who viewed himself as a magus, evoking his poems from a mystical, transcendent realm. Shakespeare, too, viewed his art in much the same light, representing himself (as scholars agree) in the figure of the magician Prospero.

That the poet's art depends on a form of wizardry – the ability to conjure enchantment from a particular combination of words – has become a critical truism. As J. A. Cuddon puts it in his authoritative dictionary of literary terms, "In the final analysis what makes a poem different from any other kind of composition is a species of magic."

Harold Schechter
Kimiko Hahn

PRESTIDIGITATION

THE MAGICIANS AT WORK

after Jim Steinmeyer's book Hiding the Elephant:
How Magicians Invented the Impossible and
Learned to Disappear

Over the years they hunted,
the wayward apprentice watchmakers,
the disappointing sons who transformed
their surnames, hunted over acres
of hinges, cogs, calluses, hidden whiskey,
mustaches a breath from feral,
poured an ocean of fortune
into fabrications of brass and iron,
spent entire seasons strumming
massive harps of wire into perfect
calibrations of invisibility,
prayed to the gods of adjustable mirrors,
cursed the gods of temperamental gaslights,
broke the legs of imitators and thieves,
chewed holes in each other's pockets,
harnessed nightmares of giant silver hoops
making endless passes over the bodies
of the dead, hoisted high a cenotaph
for hundreds of sacrificed rabbits,
breathed miles of delicate thread
into the lost labyrinths of their lungs,

all to make a woman float
to make a woman float.
and none of them ever thought
of simply asking her.

MAGIC MOUSE

Scrap of fur or fabric scrambles hand to hairy wrist,
flees into the hole thumb and forefinger make
in the fist, most warm days, Sixth Avenue and 14th Street:

big-headed guy squats hands outstretched and the toy
slips knuckle to back of the other hand, scurries to the
nest
as if of its own volition while he blares over and over

same flat vowels, somehow half the time trumping
layered horns and airbrakes and din of no apparent
origin,
raising his terms above the avenue as if he peddled

not the thing itself but its unprintable name:
MAHJIK MAOWWZ,
his accomplishment, a phrase the alphabet refuses.

MAH as in *Nah* as in *No way, JIK* the voice's arc
fallen hard back to the sidewalk, *MAOWWZZ*
a bridge with a long slide in the center. It won't work

unless you're loud, seal your nasal passages,
inflect five syllables in blat and euphony,
then the little three-syllable follow-through,

price-tag vocalise tailing away like an afterthought:
ONE DOLLAH. Even halfway down the block he's
    altered
the air, made the spine around which some fraction

of city arranges itself, his beautiful thing
in diminishing coda as you're further away:
Magic Mouse, one dahlah. I practice, I can't

get it right. Maybe what's required is resistance:
indifferent citizens impelled in four directions,
scraps of cell-phone recitations into private ethers,

mechanical sobs his syllables cut through and against.
Maybe it's the sheer persistence of the ugly span
of phrase lifting up and over what it's built to represent.

Or else the engine of his song's the nothing
that could contain that tumbling scrappy model
of a living thing in his hands,

so he says it again and again

– while the little toy, all the word
won't hold, always escaping,
goes on with its astonishing work.

18   MARK DOTY (1953–)

THE MAGIC TRICK

Half clown, half Keebler elf, he works a throng
of meth heads and young mothers who peruse
the storefronts, tugging surly kids along.
The pant legs bunch around his wingtip shoes.

When a couple walks up to his TV tray,
he hands them each a tattered business card.
"Who wants to see a magic trick today?"
He mugs and cuts a deck. His hands are scarred

but seldom shake. The two confer, agree,
and fidget as the magician fans an arc
of cherubs laced with flips of filigree.
The man inspects them for a telltale mark,

but they look clean. I've watched him do this trick
for weeks now, each time to polite surprise:
He hams it up, he lays the charm on thick;
as always, haughty jacks materialize.

The woman smiles and nods, as if content.
Another trick: He pulls a wrinkled bill
from his lapel and folds the president,
explaining how "a wise investment will

turn one buck into ten," et cetera.
He taps twice on the bill, a modest "one,"
unfolds it square by square, and then *voila!* –
the bust of Alexander Hamilton.

They clap as the magician takes a bow.
He's greasy, but he's on the up-and-up,
and magic tricks are good enough for now.
The woman floats a dollar to his cup.

THE SORCERER'S SONG

Oh! my name is JOHN WELLINGTON WELLS –
I'm a dealer in magic and spells,
    In blessings and curses,
    And ever-filled purses,
In prophecies, witches, and knells!
If you want a proud foe to "make tracks" –
If you'd melt a rich uncle in wax –
    You've but to look in
    On our resident Djinn,
Number seventy, Simmery Axe.

We've a first-class assortment of magic;
    And for raising a posthumous shade
With effects that are comic or tragic,
    There's no cheaper house in the trade.
Love-philtre – we've quantities of it;
    And for knowledge if any one burns,
We keep an extremely small prophet, a prophet
    Who brings us unbounded returns:
        For he can prophesy
        With a wink of his eye,
        Peep with security
        Into futurity,
        Sum up your history,
        Clear up a mystery,

Humour proclivity
For a nativity.
With mirrors so magical,
Tetrapods tragical,
Bogies spectacular,
Answers oracular,
Facts astronomical,
Solemn or comical,
And, if you want it, he
Makes a reduction on taking a quantity!
Oh!
If any one anything lacks,
He'll find it all ready in stacks,
If he'll only look in
On the resident Djinn,
Number seventy, Simmery Axe!

He can raise you hosts,
Of ghosts,
And that without reflectors;
And creepy things
With wings,
And gaunt and grisly spectres!
He can fill you crowds
Of shrouds,

And horrify you vastly;
 He can rack your brains
     With chains,
 And gibberings grim and ghastly.
  Then, if you plan it, he
  Changes organity
  With an urbanity,
  Full of Satanity,
  Vexes humanity
  With an inanity
  Fatal to vanity –
Driving your foes to the verge of insanity.
  Barring tautology,
  In demonology,
  'Lectro biology,
  Mystic nosology,
  Spirit philology,
  High class astrology,
  Such is his knowledge, he
Isn't the man to require an apology!
    Oh!
My name is JOHN WELLINGTON WELLS,
I'm a dealer in magic and spells,
  In blessings and curses,
  And ever-filled purses –
In prophecies, witches, and knells.
If any one anything lacks,

He'll find it all ready in stacks,
    If he'll only look in
      On the resident Djinn,
Number seventy, Simmery Axe!

24   W. S. GILBERT (1836–1911)

CARD TRICK

There is nothing so slick as a new deck of cards
tipped out of the box and fanned over a table,
facedown, slippery as panfish, little bluegills,
their backs printed like scales. "Pick a card,
any card," says the magical bachelor uncle
home for two weeks from the merchant marine,
still wearing his watch cap, black as a night
anchored off Reykjavik, a night with a few
stars of dandruff sprinkled over the wool.
Eyes merry and blue, he is eager to show off
his trick. "Take your time, take all the time
you want," he says, his big brown hand at rest
like an island pushed up, the gray thumbnail
big as a radar antenna, but the children know
to take their time, because they already sense
that this is all there ever is, or likely will be
from this uncle, one trick, the only rare treasure
he'll ever bring back from the rest of the world.

TED KOOSER (1939–)

GOD'S BREATH

If God can be said to breathe the soul
into each living thing, as he did into Adam,
then the magician we hired
for our daughter's birthday party was like God.

Before performing the rabbit-in-the-hat trick,
before pulling shiny nickels
from Emma's ears,
he got a long skinny green balloon
and stretched it like saltwater taffy,
then put his lips to its lip and blew.

And it grew and grew,
luminous and green, it grew
in its nakedness, and when it was a yard long
the magician knotted it,
and with a few deft flicks twisted it
into a dachshund – buoyant, electric, tied to a leash
of fuchsia ribbon – that bounced
along the floor, bumping after our daughter
on their walks around the house.

Weeks later, cleaning under her bed,
I coaxed it out with a broom –
a collapsed lung furred with dust.
As long as it still had some life in it,
I couldn't throw it away.

So I popped it with a pin.
And God's breath, a little puff
from elsewhere, brushed my cheek.

THE MAGICIAN

In the tent at the carnival, the magician showed us
The woman's smiling head all by itself
In a box on a table with nothing under it
Except for the mirrors I knew all about.

I'd learned about all his tricks. I understood
How he linked and unlinked nickel-plated rings
And changed the colors of silk handkerchiefs
And made a dozen sponge-balls disappear

And reappear and multiply under cups.
I was an insider. I was fourteen.
I'd read all the books I could find about magic.
I'd practiced sleight-of-hand and fooled my friends.

The dozen other people who'd been wheedled
And barked inside the canvas weren't impressed.
They watched whatever he showed them sullenly
And didn't clap, then drifted back to the midway.

I stayed behind. He was making a cigarette
Disappear one puff at a time behind a flap
Where the woman's head was now wearing a torso
And drinking beer and looking tired of him.

I said I was a magician. Could I show him
What I could do? He shrugged. With my cold deck
I did arm-turnovers and accordion shuffles,
Back-palms, one-hand cuts, and waterfalls.

He didn't say anything. His thin mustache
Was blacker than licorice and twirled to points.
His cutaway had greasepaint on the lapels.
His clip-on bowtie had sprung his cardboard collar.

Her yellow sateen dressing gown and her shoes
And stockings looked as old as the Depression.
My shirt had once belonged to my big brother
When he'd been wider. My pants stopped short of my
    socks.

He said, *What do you really want to be?*
The woman laughed and spilled her beer in the
    sawdust.

STREET MAGICIAN: NEW MARKET SQUARE, PHILADELPHIA

The hippie squints, framing us
between his thumb and forefinger.

"I'm in charge of the magic show today
and you're the audience," he yells,
shaking his long hair like fireworks.

Two kids with open mouths plunk on the steps.
A man in a suit, a family of fourteen
drift in on the pizzazz.

"Want to see how to get an audience?" he asks.
"Applaud!" He wags a forefinger at us
and bows. He pulls a floppy hat from the air.
The crowd claps like loose screws rattling in a box.

He stares us down. "Got to do better than that."
He grins. We clap again. Thunder.

Blocks away, people lift their heads to gawk at him.
"Welcome to Cincinnati," he calls to them.

With hot pretzels in paper, babies in backpacks,
kitchen implements in crackling bags, they stream,
the skeptical, the shy, the rawfaced,
reeled in on a line of sound.
Like ants at the edge of a Kool-Aid spill,
we stand for the audience.

When he has us balanced
on his tongue's sharp edge, he says
"Want to see a hippie disappear?" He winks
slyly, sizing us up for the big lie.

"Shut your eyes." We shut our eyes.
He disappears, without even passing the hat.

THE GREAT
ESCAPOLOGIST

APPENDIX

Houdini died
not

of what
he

couldn't get
out

of but
couldn't

get out
of

him.

CHORUS

Because it's closing time at the Houdini Museum
and because there are so many of us,
Bravo the Magician calls us all up on stage
and gives us bright red ribbons to wave.
He says we've seen enough straitjackets
for one Valentine's Day, says they belong
to Houdini, as do the handcuffs, and the posters,
but please not Dorothy Dietrich who's so beautiful
she makes us forget it's February outside
in Scranton, Pennsylvania.
Her silver sandals glitter in the lights.
She can catch a bullet in her mouth.
She's fearless enough to be a mother
but on stage she looks nothing like a mother.
The ribbons in our hands turn white.

HOUDINI EXPLODES FROM
THE DEPTHS, LAUGHING

At seventeen he was the wild man in a circus who
outroared and outran tigers, quitting when a heckler's
    piece of raw steak
hit him in the eye.
Later he thought it a snooze
to escape from a triple-bolted Siberian transport van
    – after all,
the guards weren't going to leap onto his shoulders,
crush his spine with their great claws and bite
    through his neck.

He challenged police to shackle him with best butcher
    steel.
They stripped him nude and searched him intimately
    for lockpicks,
and still he shucked the cuffs like jewelry. Afterward
he advertised himself as *the only conjurer in the world
who performs stark naked*! He had a powerful physique
and enjoyed showing it off.
He burst free from sealed milk cans and bear traps.
He was the Jonah man who
regurgitated himself from a whale's belly –
chewed through it like a rat, some said.
Once (just once) he was well and truly prisoned

in iron restraints and his wife, adorable Bess,
secretly tongued the key from the rose of her mouth
to his, in a deep and swooning kiss.

He was never again trapped, never bested.
When he escaped from the Chinese Water Torture
    Cell
he saved the audience too.
He exploded from the depths laughing,
and believers would scream their relief:
the wiry dance of his sly fingers,
the invincible strength of his ursine shoulders
gave them faith in their own blazing escapes.

THE CONJURER

If there's a place the mind can hide,
it's in the thick coat of the Bengal tiger
glimpsed beside the Interboro,
white as the first touch of frost
in the almond blossom. A thing like that, well,
you keep your distance. You learn to hold still.
So the men who showed, at first, would only kneel,
their guns drawn and fixed
on what they'd later call *beautiful*,
escaped, it turns out, from the temporary camp
of the New Cole Bros. Circus, not by picked locks
or from challenge cuffs, but her handler's absent craft.
Baby's breath. Infinite.
And I heard management wanted her sold,
or else forgotten, their only draw no longer worth the
    cost.
Diminishing returns, I guess. Insurance and transfer.
But then they hired locals to sweep the grounds,
hose down the cages and paint the booths,
men who'd work for very little.
Which meant between nods, or half-drunk.
Or dusties lacing PCP with whatever they can.
If I say embalming fluid, you'll cringe,
turn away. Parsley, and you'll blush.
And I'll know my luck is sung,

that the white tiger still cleans her paw
in a trailer bound for Syracuse,
where she'll sleep until noon beneath a roof
of painted-on stars. Desire is that permanent,
etched into the body the way the body remembers salt,
how muscle remembers work.
But there's an end to the imagination's reach,
a place where the mind can only hide,
and you meant to tell me of your father's stroke,
of precision and cross-stitching.
The rheumatic fever, Sparmannia, sparrow.
It's the first warm night in April,
and your shoulders are bare.
You've taken off your shoes, curled your toes
in the new grass. *Six years*, you'll say,
and two months, and I'll tell by your voice,
almost querulous, the sure sprain of wonder.
How strange and fine to get so near to it,
you'd say if someone hadn't already.
In Australia, Houdini, vaudeville conjurer,
con man and sometime medium,
stood at the edge of The Queens Bridge,
weighted with chains, the Yarra sloshing its metaphor
against the stern of twin rowboats, and listened.
For the voice, he once told Lady Doyle.
It comes as easy as stepping off a log,
but you have to wait for the voice.

So, the stage was set and, this time,
the great conjurer's buried his trick
in a boot's tongue. Curtained by the river,
he frees his hands first, then works his legs,
dislodging a corpse in the thrashing, which rises
to the expectant crowd, gooseskinned, distended.
And I can't help but read this as directive,
that the illusion made real is somehow the point,
the comedy told in reverse.
Too close, Houdini must have thought
as he climbed the wharf, cast irons glinting
in his raised left hand. Growing up,
I had a friend whose mother worked nights
at Jamaica Hospital. When her husband left them,
she took on extra shifts and fell into the habit
of collecting photographs from the emergency room,
clipped and arranged on her dining table, displayed
with the same care a conjurer's assistant
must showcase her wardrobe. We took notice,
of course, but she never said a word about them.
And though it is wrong to guess anything,
I think she, too, meant to instruct,
to steer us somewhere near the ineffable,
or the how and when of not getting it right.
Tonight, my father's been gone twelve years.
And your father's still sick. But I meant to tell you
of the Bengal tiger, how she hurt no one

and simply walked through the picnic
of a Berean missionary choir, their gathered breath,
their hosannas and awe. I wanted to say
how she came to the Interboro, immaculate,
flooded in light, and stopped there as though hitting
her mark, half-a-mile from the grave
where Houdini's body was blessed, grieved, and
    buried,
where it's almost believed, if you listen close enough,
you can even hear the dead.

Houdini, who had once escaped a steel-lined
Siberian prison van, and the maximum-security
cell that held President Garfield's assassin,
and even (like Jonah) the carcass of a whale
in which he had been sewn fast by surgeons,
could not escape death, which surprised him

in a Detroit hospital across from an ironworks
where he was pronounced dead of a ruptured
appendix on Halloween Day, 1926. In the last
minute of his life, his temperature plunged
from 104° to 84°. "That was his soul
leaving the body," his wife said to the doctor.

He was buried in Wisconsin in a bronze casket
which he had used in his final performance:
airtight and waterproof, it was submerged
in a glass tank filled with ice water,
Houdini handcuffed and manacled within.
A curtain was drawn over the tank.
Two, three, four minutes passed, and there

was no sign of him. Women screamed.
Someone pulled the fire alarm. . . .
It always went like this. Until Houdini

sauntered down the aisle from the back
of the theater and opened the curtain,
revealing the tank, empty of water, to be
filled with gold coins and the casket gone.

He had promised his wife he would send
her a message from beyond the grave.
But despite countless séances with mediums
on five continents, no message ever came.
The bust on his mausoleum was vandalized,
but his grave was left undisturbed.
So it caused a commotion one Halloween
many years after his death when the bronze
casket turned up in a Manhattan warehouse
in a cache of his other stage props.
Corroded and earth-stained, it was pried open,
and a single gold coin was discovered inside.
A woman's head, with platinum pinpoints in
her averted eyes, was embossed on the coin.

The coin was sent to the police laboratory,
but by dawn its face was smooth: the woman's
head had receded back into the gold. The casket
languished for years among the props; when it
disappeared one winter night, the temperature in
the warehouse plummeted and, despite all changes
of season, to this day remains fixed at exactly 5°.

MRS. HOUDINI

"Houdini hasn't come. I don't believe he will."
Bess Houdini, as she switched off the light by her husband's portrait,
after waiting ten years past his death for his spirit to speak.

Your trick was the longest,
to wait out those years
cuffed to his memory:
King of Magic,
Undisputed Monarch of Shackles
who slithered from slave collars,
melted through walls
while you stood beside him, smiling.

It started with a vanishing act —
first date, Coney Island.
He waved his arms,
you fled your girlhood
and in the flurry, dropped your name.
You were just what he needed,
a petite soubrette,
stockings wrinkling at the knees,
the buckled dancing shoes.
A slip of a thing,
ninety-four pounds.
How well you fit in the box.

And when his public demanded more,
the playbill artist painted
breasts, hips. Stroke by stroke,
curve by curve,
you changed into Mrs. Houdini.

Metamorphosis, his favorite act,
featured ropes, sack, and a trunk.
In a three-second switch
you slid from yourself,
became him, jacket and all.
But the time he lost the key,
how was it then, inside the trunk,
listening for the click?
The audience stirred,
leaned in their seats
while you waited,
the clock ticking,
your small feet thumping,
your breath closing in.
Of course he made it.
Always, just in time
to take his bow.

And when he vanished,
you were still here,
real as the coffin hermetically sealed,
real as the earth he denied.
Beneath his portrait you sat silent,
his old letters in your lap,
waiting his spirit's return
until the night
you switched off the light,
his heavy name
dropped from your shoulders,
and light as a girl,
you bobbed to the surface
tasting the air
while all around
the waves wove a chant —
Bess, Bess —
the spell of your natural name.

HOUDINI IN KARIS

I went to the basement on the afternoon of the
nineteenth of August and made a carpet from
galvanised three-inch nails and ice-green shards of
bottles I had thrown on the stone floor.
The audience roars when on the carpet I slowly
    stretch out
my wonderful back.
I can break out of all the strongboxes there have ever
    been.
I walk with light steps in my star-strewn slippers.
Everyone asks about my age and that the wounds
    don't bleed
I give no interviews and think in the morning
and the evening when I fall asleep about one thing.
    That one goes
up to someone and means something. That one will
    stay.
I wanted to change my life! Sometimes I think
I glimpse a beloved figure at the bus stop,
like a movement only, there was often someone else
    in a
dark blue jacket and yet we vanish in the glitter.

HOUDINI

There is a river under this poem.
It flows blue and icy
And carries these lines down the page.
Somewhere beneath its surface
Lying chained to the silt
Harry holds his breath
And slowly files
His fingernails into moons.
He wonders who still waits at the dock
If the breasts of those young girls
Have developed since he sank.
He thinks of his parents
Of listening to the tumblers
Of his mother's womb
Of escaping upward out of puberty
Out of the pupils in his father's eyes
And those hot Wisconsin fields.
He dreams of escaping from this poem
Of cracking the combinations
To his own body
And those warm young safes
Of every girl on the dock.
Jiggling his chains
Harry scares a carp that circles
And nibbles at his feet.

He feels the blue rush of the current
Sweeping across his body
Stripping his chains of their rust
Until each link softens
And glows like a tiny eel.
And Harry decides to ascend.
He slips with the water through his chains
And moving upward
Climbing over and over his own air bubbles
He waves to the fish
To his chains glittering
And squirming in the silt.
He pauses to pick a bouquet
Of seaweed for the young girls on the dock.
Rising he bursts the surface of this poem.
He listens for shouts.
He hears only the night
And a buoy sloshing in the blue.

MANZINI: ESCAPE ARTIST

now there are no bonds except the flesh; listen —
there was this boy, Manzini, stubborn with
gut stood with black tights and a turquoise
leaf across his sex

and smirking while the big
brute tied his neck arms legs, Manzini
naked waist up and white with sweat

struggled. Silent, delinquent, he
was suddenly all teeth and knee, straining slack
and excellent with sweat, inwardly

wondering if Houdini would take as long
as he; fighting time and the drenched
muscular ropes, as though his tendons were worn
on the outside —

as though his own guts were the ropes
encircling him; it was beautiful; it was thursday;
     listen —
there was this boy, Manzini

finally free, slid as snake from
his own sweet agonized skin, to throw his entrails
white upon the floor
with a cry of victory –

now there are no bonds except the flesh,
but listen, it was thursday, there was this boy,
Manzini –

HOUDINI

I suspect he knew that trunks are metaphors,
could distinguish between the finest rhythms
unrolled on rope or singing in a chain
and knew the metrics of the deepest pools

I think of him listening to the words
spoken by manacles, cells, handcuffs,
chests, hampers, roll-top desks, vaults,
especially the deep words spoken by coffins

escape, escape: quaint Harry in his suit
his chains, his desk, attached to all attachments
how he'd sweat in that precise struggle
with those binding words, wrapped around him
like that mannered style, his formal suit

and spoken when? by whom? What thing first said
"there's no way out?"; so that he'd free himself,
leap, squirm, no matter how, to chain himself again,
once more jump out of the deep alive
with all his chains singing around his feet
like the bound crowds who sigh, who sigh.

ELI MANDEL (1922–92)   53

OUT OF A STRAIT-JACKET
UPSIDE DOWN

I saw a sea of faces
Looking upward from the street
At a man who hung suspended
From a rope that bound his feet.
They were anxious, they were fearful,
They were curious, they were glad,
They were laughing, they were tearful,
They were joyous, they were sad.

High above them he was swinging,
With a jacket round him tied;
He was wriggling, he was twisting,
As he tried to get outside.
Just a few immortal minutes
And his arms were free, and then,
He threw out his hands in greeting,
And they brought him down again.

And in all that throng beholding
His agility, his skill –
Watched him dangling in the ether
While their very hearts stood still –
There were many in strait-jackets
That I thought they'd like to cast

As Houdini did that moment,
And to feel them free at last.

For life binds all in clutches,
And in gyves and jackets, too.
And we'd like to get outside them,
Even in the public view —
Like to get outside our errors,
Get outside our habits vain,
And be free from wicked terrors,
And be happy men again.

HOUDINI

Each escape
involved some art,
some hokum, and
at least a brief
incomprehensible
exchange between
man and metal
during which the
chains were not
so much broken
as he and they
blended. At the
end of each such
mix he had to
extract himself. It
was the hardest
part to get right
routinely: breaking
back into the
same Houdini.

HOUDINI IN A BARREL

Death cannot chain him with its roots of earth,
with mortal padlocks of steel crafted deft and sure,
because this is Houdini, capable of becoming as new
as a changed name, slipping cuffs cinched at the wrist,
divining the gears that would lower til they raise
  him up,
breaking the bounds of belief and reason, without
  a sweat,
without any evidence given of his gnawing from a
  trap,
sawtoothed blades in the oxygenless dark, cutting,
  clawing,
scraping, prying his way out of any box that would
  pound the ear
by a clockarm's striking of time, to laugh at the
  dumbfounded
when he escapes from each river's current pulling
  inexorably down,
because this is Houdini, the one who would look hard
  in Death's face.

BRIAN TURNER (1967−)   57

WIZARDRY

ST. DUNSTAN AND THE WORD OF POWER

St. Dunstan stood again in his tower, Alembic,
crucible, all complete; He had been standing a good
half hour, And now he utter'd the words of power,
And call'd to his Broomstick to bring him a seat.

The words of power! – and what be they To which
e'en Broomsticks bow and obey? – Why, – 'twere
uncommonly hard to say, As the prelate I named
has recorded none of them, What they may be, But
I know they are three, And ABRACADABRA, I take it,
is one of them: For I'm told that most Cabalists use
that identical Word, written thus in what they call "a
Pentacle."

However that be, You'll doubtless agree It signifies
little to you or to me, As not being dabblers in
Grammarye; Still, it must be confess'd, for a Saint to
repeat Such language aloud is scarcely discreet.

RICHARD HARRIS BARHAM (1788–1845)   61

THE BROKEN STRING

Nuing-kuiten my father's friend
was a lion sorcerer
and walked on feet of hair.
People saw his spoor and said:
"The sorcerer has visited us.
He is the one who treads on hair.
This big animal prowling
was Nuing-kuiten."

He used to travel by night –
he did not want to be seen
for people might shoot at him
and he might maul someone.
At night he could go unseen,
after other lion sorcerers
who slink into our dwellings
and drag out men.

The sorcerer lived with us
hunting in a lion's form
until an ox fell prey to him.
Then the Boers rode out
and shot my father's friend,
but he fought those people off

and came home to tell father
how Boers had wounded him.

He thought father did not know
he was wounded in his lion form.
Soon he would have to go
for he lay in extreme pain.
If only he could take father
and teach him his magic and songs,
father would walk in his craft,
sing his songs, and remember him.
He died, and my father sang:

"Men broke the string for me
and made my dwelling like this.
Men broke the string for me
and now
my dwelling is strange to me.

My dwelling stands empty
because the string has broken,
and now
my dwelling is a hardship for me."

DIAKWAIN (c. 1845–76)   63
TRANSLATED BY HAROLD FARMER

"BEST WITCHCRAFT IS GEOMETRY"

Best Witchcraft is Geometry
To the magician's mind –
His ordinary acts are feats
To thinking of mankind.

A CHARM
from *The Indian Emperor*

Thou Moon, that aidest us with thy magic might,
And ye small stars, the scattered seeds of light,
Dart your pale beams into this gloomy place,
That the sad powers of the infernal race
May read above what's hid from human eyes,
And in your walks see empires fall and rise.

And ye immortal souls, who once were men,
And now resolved to elements again,
Who wait for mortal frames in depths below,
And did before what we are doomed to now;
Once, twice, and thrice I wave my sacred wand,
Ascend – ascend – ascend, at my command.

JOHN DRYDEN (1631 – 1700)   65

RUNE OF THE FINLAND WOMAN
for Sára Karig

"You are so wise," the reindeer said, "you can bind the winds of the world in a single strand."

H. C. Andersen, *The Snow Queen*

She could bind the world's winds in a single strand.
She could find the world's words in a singing wind.
She could lend a weird will to a mottled hand.
She could wind a willed word from a muddled mind.

She could wend the wild woods on a saddled hind.
She could sound a wellspring with a rowan wand.
She could bind the wolf's wounds in a swaddling band.
She could bind a banned book in a silken skin.

She could spend a world war on invaded land.
She could pound the dry roots to a kind of bread.
She could feed a road gang on invented food.
She could find the spare parts of the severed dead.

She could find the stone limbs in a waste of sand.
She could stand the pit cold with a withered lung.
She could handle bad puns in the slang she learned.
She could dandle foundlings in their mother tongue.

She could plait a child's hair with a fishbone comb.
She could tend a coal fire in the Arctic wind.
She could mend an engine with a sewing pin.
She could warm the dark feet of a dying man.

She could drink the stone soup from a doubtful well.
She could breathe the green stink of a trench latrine.
She could drink a queen's share of important wine.
She could think a few things she would never tell.

She could learn the hand code of the deaf and blind.
She could earn the iron keys of the frozen queen.
She could wander uphill with a drunken friend.
She could bind the world's winds in a single strand.

MARILYN HACKER (1942–)

FAUSTUS' DESIRE

These metaphysics of magicians,
And necromantic books, are heavenly.
Lines, circles, letters, characters:
Aye, these are those that Faustus most desires.
O what a world of profit and delight,
Of power, of honour, and omnipotence,
Is promised to the studious artizan!
All things that move between the quiet poles
Shall be at my command. Emperors and kings
Are but obey'd in their several provinces;
But his dominion that exceeds in this,
Stretcheth as far as doth the mind of man:
A sound magician is a demigod.
Here tire my brains to get a deity.

MERLIN

O Merlin in your crystal cave
Deep in the diamond of the day,
Will there ever be a singer
Whose music will smooth away
The furrow drawn by Adam's finger
Across the meadow and the wave?
Or a runner who'll outrun
Man's long shadow driving on,
Break through the gate of memory
And hang the apple on the tree?
Will your magic ever show
The sleeping bride shut in her bower,
The day wreathed in its mound of snow
And Time locked in his tower?

EDWIN MUIR (1887–1959)

RIDDLES OF MERLIN

As I was walking
   Alone by the sea,
"What is that whisper?"
   Said Merlin to me.
"Only," I answered,
   "The sigh of the wave" –
"Oh, no," replied Merlin,
   " 'Tis the grass on your grave."

As I lay dreaming
   In churchyard ground
"Listen," said Merlin,
   "What is that sound?"
"The green grass is growing,"
   I answered; but he
Chuckled, *"Oh, no!*
   'Tis the sound of the sea."

As I went homeward
   At dusk by the shore,
"What is that crimson?"
   Said Merlin once more.
"Only the sun," I said.
   "Sinking to rest" –
"Sunset for East," he said,
   "Sunrise for West."

70   ALFRED NOYES (1880–1958)

THE WIZARD'S CHANT

I sit and beat the wizard's magic drum;
And by its mystic sound I call the beasts.
From mountain lair and forest nook they throng;
E'en mighty storms obey the dreadful sound.

I sit and beat the wizard's magic drum;
The storm and thunder answer when it calls.
Aplasemwesit, mighty whirlwind, stops
To hearken to the mystic sound I make.

I sit and beat the wizard's magic drum;
And Chibela'kwe, night-air spirit, flies
To hearken to the mystic sound I make;
And old Wu'cho'sen, storm-bird of the North,
Rests his great pinions, causing calm to reign,
To hearken to the mystic sound I make.

I sit and beat the wizard's magic drum;
And Lumpeguin, who dwells beneath the wave,
Arises to the surface struck with awe,
To hearken to the mystic sound I make.

E'en Atwuskniges, armed with axe of stone,
Will cease his endless chopping, and be still
To hearken to the mystic sound I make.

I sit and beat the wizard's magic drum;
And Appodumken, with his long, red hair,
Ariseth from the depths, and draweth near
To hearken to the mystic sound I make.

The lightning, thunder, storm and forest sprite,
The whirlwind, gale, and spirit of the deep,
The Chibela'kwe, loathly night-air ghost,
All come together, and with reverent mien
Will hearken to the mystic sound I make.

TRANSLATED BY CHARLES GODFREY LELAND
and JOHN DYNELLY PRINCE

WITCH WIFE

I'll conjure the perfect Easter
& we'll plant mini spruces in the yard –
my pink gloves & your green gloves

like parrots from an opera over the earth –
We'll chatter about our enemies' spectacular deaths.
I'll conjure the perfect Easter

dark pesto sauce sealed with lemon
long cords of fusilli to remind you of my hair
& my pink gloves. Your gloves are green

& transparent like the skin of Christ
when He returned, filmed over with moss roses –
I'll conjure as perfect an Easter:

provolone cut from the whole ball
woody herbs burning our tongues – it's a holiday
I conjure with my pink and green gloves

wrangling life from the dirt. It all turns out
as I'd hoped. The warlocks of winter are dead
& it's Easter. I dig up body after body after body
with my pink gloves, my green gloves.

KIKI PETROSINO (1979–)   73

PROSPERO ABJURES HIS MAGIC
from *The Tempest*

Ye elves of hills, brooks, standing lakes and groves,
And ye that on the sands with printless foot
Do chase the ebbing Neptune and do fly him
When he comes back; you demi-puppets that
By moonshine do the green sour ringlets make,
Whereof the ewe not bites, and you whose pastime
Is to make midnight mushrooms, that rejoice
To hear the solemn curfew; by whose aid,
Weak masters though ye be, I have bedimm'd
The noontide sun, call'd forth the mutinous winds,
And 'twixt the green sea and the azured vault
Set roaring war: to the dread rattling thunder
Have I given fire and rifted Jove's stout oak
With his own bolt; the strong-based promontory
Have I made shake and by the spurs pluck'd up
The pine and cedar: graves at my command
Have waked their sleepers, oped, and let 'em forth
By my so potent art. But this rough magic
I here abjure, and, when I have required
Some heavenly music, which even now I do,
To work mine end upon their senses that
This airy charm is for, I'll break my staff,
Bury it certain fathoms in the earth,
And deeper than did ever plummet sound
I'll drown my book.

74   WILLIAM SHAKESPEARE (1564–1616)

MERLIN

For Merlin had in magic more insight
Than ever him before or after living wight:

For he by words could call out of the sky
Both sun and moon, and make them him obey;
The land to sea, and sea to mainland dry,
And darksome night he eke could turn to day;
Huge hosts of men he could alone dismay,
And hosts of men of meanest things could frame,
Whenso him list his enemies to fray:
That to this day for terror of his fame,
The fiends do quake when any him to them does
    name.

from "MERLIN AND THE GLEAM"

I.

O Young Mariner,
You from the haven
Under the sea-cliff,
You that are watching
The gray Magician
With eyes of wonder,
I am Merlin,
And *I* am dying,
I am Merlin
Who follow The Gleam.

II.

Mighty the Wizard
Who found me at sunrise
Sleeping, and woke me
And learn'd me Magic!
Great the Master,
And sweet the Magic,
When over the valley,
In early summers,
Over the mountain,

On human faces,
And all around me,
Moving to melody,
Floated The Gleam.

III.

Once at the croak of a Raven who crost it,
A barbarous people,
Blind to the magic,
And deaf to the melody,
Snarl'd at and cursed me.
A demon vext me,
The light retreated,
The landskip darken'd,
The melody deaden'd,
The Master whisper'd
"Follow The Gleam."

ALFRED, LORD TENNYSON (1809–92)   77

THE MAGUS

The pearls, mere reminders.
The ocean's rapid recoil, a signal.
The gulls appeared enormous

in that way only things from above can –
such is presentation of the sudden.
If only this were worthy of a frame,

the wooden gesture announcing
a moment past were cherished.
But it was too late for that, too late

to answer the surf's anxious *Why?*
too late to decline the continuous life
he had resigned himself, turning

away from the grave, that plot
being too familiar to so many.
Of course immortality had its price:

first his staff he had taped back together,
then the sleeves of his robe
he had reclaimed from the depths, then

the magic leached nightly from his fingertips
so that now his incantation for a storm
brought only a slight breeze,

a quick sun shower that frightened
only the flowers struggling in the salt air.
Now, showing his centuries, he insists:

This is the wind out of which I bring clouds.
These are my hands that gnarled though they be
when lifted to the sky bring rain.

C. DALE YOUNG (1969–)   79

THE MAGICIAN'S
ASSISTANT

THE MAGICIAN'S GIRL

This is what will be left of me
when I die: bones, slices of body, two parts

that will never reconcile. Halved in a box,
all spangles and boas, my fringed gold skirt.

Handfuls of dirt, glitter, a feather. I will
remember a saw in midair, light-struck,

how my legs spun from my arms, the round
of applause. The magician who tapped

the air, my rise from smoke. This is where
it will all end: stage and magic, canary flutter,

someone's awful scream. Later, the mirror,
the dressing room, the cotton ball stained.

Graveside, even my skin is a prop —
the harlequin scarves

of my voice still trapped up his sleeve.

AMANDA AUCHTER (1977 –)   83

THE PUPIL IN MAGIC

I am now, – what joy to hear it! –
  Of the old magician rid;
And henceforth shall ev'ry spirit
  Do whate'er by me is bid;
    I have watch'd with rigour
      All he used to do,
    And will now with vigour
      Work my wonders too.

Wander, wander
  Onward lightly,
  So that rightly
    Flow the torrent,
And with teeming waters yonder
    In the bath discharge its current!

And now come, thou well-worn broom,
  And thy wretched form bestir;
Thou hast ever served as groom,
  So fulfil my pleasure, sir!

On two legs now stand,
  With a head on top;
Waterpail in hand,
  Haste, and do not stop!

Wander, wander
    Onward lightly,
    So that rightly
        Flow the torrent,
And with teeming waters yonder
        In the bath discharge its current!

See! he's running to the shore,
    And has now attain'd the pool,
And with lightning speed once more
    Comes here, with his bucket full!
        Back he then repairs;
            See how swells the tide!
        How each pail he bears
            Straightway is supplied!

    Stop, for, lo!
        All the measure
        Of thy treasure
            Now is right! —
    Ah, I see it! woe, oh woe!
        I forget the word of might.

Ah, the word whose sound can straight
    Make him what he was before!
Ah, he runs with nimble gait!
    Would thou wert a broom once more!

Streams renew'd for ever
    Quickly bringeth he;
River after river
    Rusheth on poor me!

Now no longer
    Can I bear him;
I will snare him,
    Knavish sprite!
Ah, my terror waxes stronger!
    What a look! what fearful sight!

Oh, thou villain child of hell!
    Shall the house through thee be drown'd?
Floods I see that wildly swell,
    O'er the threshold gaining ground.
        Wilt thou not obey,
            Oh, thou broom accurs'd?
        Be thou still, I pray,
            As thou wert at first!

Will enough
    Never please thee?
I will seize thee,
    Hold thee fast,
And thy nimble wood so tough,
    With my sharp axe split at last.

See, once more he hastens back!
  Now, oh Cobold, thou shalt catch it!
    I will rush upon his track;
  Crashing on him falls my hatchet.
      Bravely done, indeed!
        See, he's cleft in twain!
      Now from care I'm freed,
        And can breathe again.

    Woe, oh woe!
      Both the parts,
      Quick as darts,
        Stand on end,
    Servants of my dreaded foe!
        Oh, ye gods, protection send!

And they run! and wetter still
  Grow the steps and grows the hall.
  Lord and master, hear me call!
Ever seems the flood to fill,
      Ah, he's coming! see,
        Great is my dismay!
      Spirits raised by me
        Vainly would I lay!

"To the side
  Of the room
  Hasten, broom,
    As of old!
Spirits I have ne'er untied
    Save to act as they are told."

THE SORCERER'S APPRENTICE

The old man is full of tricks.

He can fill the gutter with soup.
His jinx bent the stones of the hall
to an arch tonight. The walls lean silent,
gloomy with the power of words.

That's his book on the table.

> *The sea will come*
> *when I call,*
> *the sea will rise*
> *and flower this shore*
> *with the energy of wolves*

This time I got it. The stony floor's
a tide pool. The clams are spouting.
Now I conjure a redwood grove around the room,
now I wave the walls high and vanish the roof for
    moonlight!

But I hear a wind turn in the light
where the roof used to be.
It circles down the walls like a vulture;
the trees tangle slow, like vines.

The master is awake, of course.
In the vault above us the moon reddens like a red
     pencil.
The wind makes a sound like strangling
and the roof shuts.

THE MAGICIAN'S ASSISTANT

The first night he sawed me in half
I expected a trick – another girl

huddled in the stage-left end
of the polished cabinet,

waiting to poke out her toes
while I smiled, unworried,

from the opposite side.
Once we both were clear, I imagined,

he'd lift the rhinestone-handled saw
and slice the air between us,

faking the work it would take
to cut through a body.

But then he opened the golden lid
and there wasn't a trick, wasn't

a girl. Just pine boards,
splintered and bare. All the same,

when he took my hand
I climbed in. I'd seen his act

over and over, other chicks
in the same short sequined dress,

smiling at their own feet
from across the stage. As tricks go

it's hardly rare – we've all cheered
a man who wouldn't be sated

with a single cut, who'd slice a woman
in half, then halve each half again.

How did I grin through that pain?
A wave of his wand

and I was whole again. Scarless.
I didn't ask how. Six nights a week

for two years, he broke me apart,
put me together. *Just like new,*

he bragged – never pausing
even once to look – then took his bow.

92   PHILIP MEMMER (1971–)

MY MAGICIAN

Someone pulled me out of a tux sleeve,
Doctor, hanging for my dear life
At the end of a long white scarf.
I fluttered over my magician.
I flew around the hushed theater.

Saturdays, at nine and at midnight,
He sawed me in half,
While I lay in the coffin
Next to my naked bride.
I never got to see his face
Even when the applause started.

We held our breaths under his hat.
Two look-alike dummies, we took
Turns sitting on his knee.
Through a row of wooden teeth
We spoke of God the Father.
Then we vanished in a pack of cards.

We were terrified and happy.
One instant he was swallowing fire,
The next he was spitting it
With the two of us riding the long flame
Like a coach into the sunset.

Between his tricks I was nowhere
I could think of:
Not in this world with its chained bear
And its magic mirror,
Not in that other
Where the white clouds float and sheep graze.

LIVES OF THE
MAGICIANS

THE MAGICIAN

i.

Its else, to them, lets logic spill through. Upend,
suspend what they no longer want to be real,
return them to credulity and they'll shill
the very silk from their souls to keep "prudent" pretend.
I knew this from, perhaps, five. Before
radio, before film, before even inconsequence,
I was drawn to it, magic, that boyish lore
conjured into career. When, then, did I chance

to peak, Iowa? There are signs, always, one should
     doubt
one's own tales, the blunderbuss trussed up as history.
Yes, I tramped the world at twelve, could count
the Bard a shard in my repertoire a good while
before that, graced the stage at three, knew Houdini
even, but nothing charmed charms for long, not gaud,
     not Grover's Mill.

ii.

Nothing charmed stays charmed for long; not God,
not Grover's Mill. But when the audience
wants little green men, the film of the century,
an aunt who bathes in Perrier only to disappear

one Sunday in a rickshaw in China,
when they beg for a genius, misunderstood
of course, slugging his way through poverty
hawking cheap wine, when the hag-massed conscience

of the country demands the odd, you nod,
smile, trick up your sleeve and give it the good
Tinsel Town try. Not that Vaudeville ranks minor
billing on the tally sheet of the Grand Exchequer.
It's just that, well, each stage we've built stands for
    having stood;
there's no more holy in holly than promises in wood.

iii.

There's no more holy in holly than there's promise
in the sky. I knew this that Halloween,
knew the last best hoax was my own faith
in nothing, but still the sky fell for the poor
rubes who would have bought whatever precipice,
bridgeless, I sold them. I took them in their green
years, hobbled them with hope, fed them the wraith
they were already ready to swallow. *Bore*

no one. Like lightning, that maxim led me,
all fire, fume, forked finesse, into each
irradiated rec-room, from boondocks to beach.

And there, they dangled for me, plunged to the sea.
Philco or fife, magic or Martian or holy shroud . . .
Lord! Blackstone, Barnum, they would've been proud.

iv.

Lord Blackstone, old Barnum, both would've been
    proud.
There was that woman, poison in hand, they found
locked in her bathroom, her children huddled
in the tub. "They're coming," was all the muddled
confession they could wring from her. Gas, hunger,
    death
lobbed by tripod heat ray, the threat of each new breath
breathed beneath some suppurating Martian thumb . . .
Hundreds fled the cities believing the end had come.

Switchboards caught fire, the streets swarmed, police
    collected
in night's crotch to clutch at what they once protected,
blue ticks worrying a dog worrying his long dead
master's thigh. They clamored for treats, receipts for
    dread
that no one — Hirohito, Hitler — had the balls yet to
    redeem.
Magicians know at least this trick: Sustain the waking
    dream.

v.

Magicians. Know. Least. Each word a trick
to sustain, a waking dream that, once silent,
became radio, movies, me. See, I could
never keep my own trap shut. So I took some
of the fallen with me, so what? It's not
as if I'd knotted the not myself around
each pale fruit, each mottled neck just to see
how some sad sap troped his rope's end. No, the kick

I got, I got from what they all thought was meant
for them only. Yes, I provided gopher wood
and hammer, hope, apocalyptic yammer. Dumb
beasts, we always believe we'll leave behind our lot.
Truth is, no matter if we hang, drown, flee,
someone's box awaits us, always, false wall down.

vi.

Someone's box awaits us, always, false wall down.
Divided by boards, sometimes swords, mirrors,
compartments within compartments, secret
hollows behind a screen, the smoke between
us and everything else that clearly isn't
keeps our demons baying and at bay. Horrors,
bullroarers, God's command to leave for Nineveh,
Jack-o-lanterns, the will of each wisp, swamp gas,

crabgrass, Barnum's termited giant, Piltdown
Man, combustible bushes . . . Pumpkins remain
pumpkins, no matter how we slice them. Ask
for fear and unto you it shall be – Given
this, this frenzy, envy, obsession to be awed,
is it any wonder what we've sought, this box, this sod?

vii.

Is it any wonder that we've sought to box
our God between reels, that we've looked for each
next-best messiah in the dark? No director,
no writer worth a damn ever let that urge
rest. Give a guy the world's largest erector
set and, if he owns to that smirch of demiurge
born in the blood, he's got no choice. Reach.
We all want rabbits, hats. We plunge our arms

deep into that deep to steal the little
of Leviathan we dare, borrowing what rocks
faith founders on to build our house of charms –
theater, we call it, show – and here, each rosed bud
promises garden, Hava even, precious metal
of all else, letting logic spill through, unopened.

THE MAGICIAN'S DREAM

I pull this from nowhere, from
    out of the hips of roses,
        from the scar

in the sky. It is this,
    what I'm holding, what you can't see,
        this lovely piece

of thisness, this body of wild claim
    I'd like you to care about.
        Imagine this, for example.

Or imagine this: earthlight bottled
    in a factory near Newark and sold
        to the stars. What I have here

is the commodity of our time, *none
    of the above*, that which always follows
        simple A,B,C, like cruelty.

It is none of your business either.
    That's why there's a possibility
        you'll care about it, this shadow

wearing a cloak in a grey world, this
    self-cancelling mandrake root
        that will not produce

a single birth. I hold it up to you now
    so that you won't see it.
        Look, it's gone

and all this time you haven't left
    your seats. Confess. All you ever cared about
        was me.

TAROT: THE MAGICIAN CARD

Rain wets the wand, wind moves a sword,
lightning lights crystal where the thundering cup
forms me a channel and takes on a word,
pouring the pentacle I gather up.
Time carves the storm in the palm of my hand,
till it fills with shapes that send me down
through my river-body. Do I stand
at a table the waiting planet surrounds?
Through my own fingers, eyes, and palm,
and through other worlds, huge or small,
one fury spins and turns me calm;
I breathe and watch it land and fall,
holding what I hardly know or see,
filled with the storm that makes, makes me.

PROLOGUE FOR A MAGICIAN

Dear victims, kindly bear with me a minute:
You see this hat? There's not one rabbit in it.
Observe these pockets? Not a bit of money
In any of them, and it's far from funny;
Moreover, as I trust you will believe,
There's positively nothing up the sleeve.

So, should I conjure kings and queens and aces
And even coins from unaccustomed places,
Or should I do extraordinary things
With handkerchiefs and ribbons, balls and rings,
Should objects come to sight that were not there
And subsequently vanish into air,
Such miracles must find their explanation
In Magic or in Prestidigitation.

Now watch me. You can do it if you try;
The quickness of the hand deceives the eye!

ARTHUR GUITERMAN (1871–1943)   105

THE MAGICIAN

The magician was a soulful man, quick rather than
    deep.
He always gave you the feeling that he knew more
than he was letting on about the audience and how
tempting it had been to bend them to his will,
though he didn't – he would rather absent himself
than play the poor man's Mussolini. So he took off,
not often but a lot, staying away just long enough
    to make
his reappearance go unremarked. He spent months
preparing for each transition, switching identities
with wigs and false noses. He wanted to be known
by no one but the dog walking beside him into
    the woods,
where a No Swimming sign means you can be
    pretty sure
people are swimming. Old conversations replayed
    themselves
in his mind. Every third sentence began "To be honest
with you," suggesting a general rule of falsehood.
The past was a hotel. The room was empty. The door
was open. He stepped in the door. There was no door.

106   DAVID LEHMAN (1948–)

THE MAGICIAN'S EXIT WOUND

All day
the sky has the look of dirty paper.
My shadow stays indoors.
I watch its step,

and plan my tricks.
This evening,
the loneliness of disappearing acts!
I think of

poking my head through the sky,
and, in those frozen pressures,
of breaking into
blood on a cloud.

from POEMS BY THE MAGICIAN

The woodwork's musty as the russet smell of old
    burnt toast and almonds.
The feather-hands
Of the falcon-clock have stopped.
                      There are no sounds,
Except the old creaking rocking-throne that stands
In a corner (still rocking, for kings and queens have
    ghosts called Histories).
                Ends
Of cowboys' cattle-brands
Hang on a wall.
         The table's one leg bends
Like a toad-stool stalk.
                The magician never mends
His old things. He never sends
Them to auction-sales, bazaars or jumble-sales.
    Indeed, he intends
To keep his attic cluttered with peaceful rubbish,
    quieter than islands.
The air is still with the dust of grated diamonds.
The feather-hands
Of the falcon-clock have stopped.
                He finds

Old things are good for games of memories, and
    sometimes he stands
For hours staring at wands –
For this is where he keeps them, old, splintered,
    broken worn-out wizard-wands.

THE MAGICIAN

Always above, on a stair, in a tower,
    the diamond-eyed magician treads the air,
and dabbles in the witchcraft of perfection,
    waving wands, batons of ideation,
he reasons, rich and rash as all heretics,
    and plains a song as pure as mathematics

At flawless dawn he rises, like the wind,
    unreels the murky crystal of the mind
to catch the sun with dappled eloquence,
    unsheathes the shady snakes of idle sense
and drives them into shining-shafted logic,
    the source and sorcerer of honest magic.

His art is long who wakes at dawn to see
    the evolution of a single day.
He fools the time that dawdles in a clock,
    and plans enchantment for a lasting trick.
In castled air and guarded by a moat
    his magic moves canonic with the light;

But light as air, the wilful conjurer
    instructs his art at night to disappear.
No dying cadence clutters permanence;
    he keeps his craft as wise as innocence,

to rise again with every crafty dawn,
    with tower and stair and reason to begin.

So magic ever was a morning vision!
    Up at six, the diamond-eyed magician
will burn through all the elemental dark
    and strike the sulfur spirit like a spark,
and shake the genii of our bottled sleep,
    and wake us like the wizardry of hope.

THE FORTUNETELLER

She stole the calling as a girl through a peephole
into the healer's hut, then practiced on Florica,
the cow with eyes like mine. Technique came later,
in a psych ward where, stunned by this unhinged
stenographer's knack for decoding her sisters'
nocturnal gibberish, the director, a former patient,
diagnosed her as prescient and, over pots of Turkish
    coffee,
transferred techniques for which he, spirit-deaf, had
    no use.
Soon her one-room flat replaced the town's
    confessional,
its doorbell a 24/7 hope dispenser.
Folk want someone to know their troubles so bad, she'd
    mutter,
they're ready to trade their shoes for a bit of listening.
I grew unashamed of hearing, accustomed
to the blueblack flesh of midnight callers.

This winter, same age as when she bartered
her brokenness, I hold the raddled deck.
We pass the dusk of my forty-sixth birthday
alone, she and I, in a chapel agloat with the agony
of the damned and angels alarmingly pokerfaced.
My galoshes, damp with transatlantic sweat,

cling to the ice-clad floor. Just this one time,
I promise myself as I shuffle the cards
on her chest, and only to see
if the cobbler will be there to resole her shoes.

MIHAELA MOSCALIUC (1972–)

THE MAGICIAN

He calls it up. It shudders and begins.
What does? The Other; all that he is not
comes into being. And the whole being turns
a sudden face, far realer than he thought.

Magician, oh endure, endure, endure!
Make equilibrium. Stand upon one scale
with all you own, and let the far side bear
It, growing to decision or denial.

The spell takes hold. He knows the scales have tipped,
the call weighs heavier. Yet his face, as though
its hour-hand and minute- overlapped,
has stopped at midnight. He is spell-bound too.

114   RAINER MARIA RILKE (1875 – 1926)
TRANSLATED BY STEPHEN MITCHELL

THE MAGICIAN'S LAST BOW

You've seen the tricks of my trade:
From the simple white rabbit
Plucked from a hat, the snipped ribbon
Unrolled back whole again to water
Poured into a glass deeper
Than a well and the usual macaw
Transformed into a dove.
That was my first routine followed
By my trim lady sawn into half,
Reborn whole to blow you a kiss
And the man locked into a closet
Resurrected amongst you in the crowd.
Now you know him to be a twin
And all the other tricks made perfect
After honing my skills to beat the blink
Of an eye, to make you believe in
Fleeting miracles – that was my mission.
Accomplished when you left, your feet
Afloat, your head light as a balloon.

Magic was a figment of my childhood.
It's only work and practice made perfect.
Now I have nothing left, nothing as
Enthralling as making a train
Vanish or for me to rise unchained

From a drowned cage or to levitate
(The transparent twine lost in the lights).
I'm a magician, not a druid or wizard.
I do not bend a spoon with my
Magnetic will. If for a moment
You fell under my spell and believed
In make-believe, I will consider my life
Well spent and privileged. But allow me,
My faithful patrons, my friends
My last act before I leave your
Presence. Watch closely now
For the end of all my illusions.
Look, with a snap of my wrist,
A flap of this black shroud
And a cloud of smoke

I no longer exist.

THE MIND-READER
Lui parla.
for Charles and Eula

Some things are truly lost. Think of a sun-hat
Laid for the moment on a parapet
While three young women – one, perhaps, in
     mourning –
Talk in the crenellate shade. A slight wind plucks
And budges it; it scuffs to the edge and cartwheels
Into a giant view of some description:
Haggard escarpments, if you like, plunge down
Through mica shimmer to a moss of pines
Amidst which, here or there, a half-seen river
Lobs up a blink of light. The sun-hat falls,
With what free flirts and stoops you can imagine,
Down through that reeling vista or another,
Unseen by any, even by you or me.
It is as when a pipe-wrench, catapulted
From the jounced back of a pick-up truck, dives
     headlong
Into a bushy culvert; or a book
Whose reader is asleep, garbling the story,
Glides from beneath a steamer chair and yields
Its flurried pages to the printless sea.

It is one thing to escape from consciousness
As such things do, another to be pent
In the dream-cache or stony oubliette
Of someone's head.
                              They found, when I was little,
That I could tell the place of missing objects.
I stood by the bed of a girl, or the frayed knee
Of an old man whose face was lost in shadow.
When did you miss it?, people would be saying,
Where did you see it last? And then those voices,
Querying or replying, came to sound
Like cries of birds when the leaves race and whiten
And a black overcast is shelving over.
The mind is not a landscape, but if it were
There would in such case be a tilted moon
Wheeling beyond the wood through which you
        groped,
Its fine spokes breaking in the tangled thickets.
There would be obfuscations, paths which turned
To dried-up stream-beds, hemlocks which invited
Through shiny clearings to a groundless shade;
And yet in a sure stupor you would come
At once upon dilapidated cairns,
Abraded moss, and half-healed blazes leading
To where, around the turning of a fear,
The lost thing shone.
                              Imagine a railway platform –

The long cars come to a cloudy halt beside it,
And the fogged windows offering a view
Neither to those within nor those without.
Now, in the crowd – forgive my predilection –
Is a young woman standing amidst her luggage,
Expecting to be met by you, a stranger.
See how she turns her head, the eyes engaging
And disengaging, pausing and shying away.
It is like that with things put out of mind,
As the queer saying goes: a lost key hangs
Trammeled by threads in what you come to see
As the webbed darkness of a sewing-basket,
Flashing a little; or a photograph,
Misplaced in an old ledger, turns its bled
Oblivious profile to rebuff your vision,
Yet glistens with the fixative of thought.
What can be wiped from memory? Not the least
Meanness, obscenity, humiliation,
Terror which made you clench your eyes, or pulse
Of happiness which quickened your despair.
Nothing can be forgotten, as I am not
Permitted to forget.

               It was not far
From that to this – this corner café table
Where, with my lank grey hair and vatic gaze,
I sit and drink at the receipt of custom.
They come here, day and night, so many people:

Sad women of the quarter, dressed in black,
As to a black confession; blinking clerks
Who half-suppose that Taurus ruminates
Upon their destinies; men of affairs
Down from Milan to clear it with the magus
Before they buy or sell some stock or other;
My fellow-drunkards; fashionable folk,
Mocking and ravenously credulous,
And skeptics bent on proving me a fraud
For fear that some small wonder, unexplained,
Should leave a fissure in the world, and all
Saint Michael's host come flapping back.

                                      I give them

Paper and pencil, turn away and light
A cigarette, as you have seen me do;
They write their questions; fold them up; I lay
My hand on theirs and go into my frenzy,
Raising my eyes to heaven, snorting smoke,
Lolling my head as in the fumes of Delphi,
And then, with shaken, spirit-guided fingers,
Set down the oracle. All that, of course,
Is trumpery, since nine times out of ten
What words float up within another's thought
Surface as soon in mine, unfolding there
Like paper flowers in a water-glass.
In the tenth case, I sometimes cheat a little.
That shocks you? But consider: what I do

Cannot, so most conceive, be done at all,
And when I fail, I am a charlatan
Even to such as I have once astounded –
Whereas a tailor can mis-cut my coat
And be a tailor still. I tell you this
Because you know that I have the gift, the burden.
Whether or not I put my mind to it,
The world usurps me ceaselessly; my sixth
And never-resting sense is a cheap room
Black with the anger of insomnia,
Whose wall-boards vibrate with the mutters, plaints,
And flushings of the race.

                        What should I tell them?
I have no answers. *Set your fears at rest,*
I scribble when I must. *Your paramour*
Is faithful, and your spouse is unsuspecting.
You were not seen, that day, beneath the fig-tree.
Still, be more cautious. When the time is ripe,
Expect promotion. I foresee a message
From a far person who is rich and dying.
You are admired in secret. If, in your judgment,
Profit is in it, you should take the gamble.
As for these fits of weeping, they will pass.

It makes no difference that my lies are bald
And my evasions casual. It contents them
Not to have spoken, yet to have been heard.

What more do they deserve, if I could give it,
Mute breathers as they are of selfish hopes
And small anxieties? Faith, justice, valor,
All those reputed rarities of soul
Confirmed in marble by our public statues –
You may be sure that they are rare indeed
Where the soul mopes in private, and I listen.
Sometimes I wonder if the blame is mine,
If through a sullen fault of the mind's ear
I miss a resonance in all their fretting.
Is there some huge attention, do you think,
Which suffers us and is inviolate,
To which all hearts are open, which remarks
The sparrow's weighty fall, and overhears
In the worst rancor a deflected sweetness?
I should be glad to know it.
                              Meanwhile, saved
By the shrewd habit of concupiscence,
Which, like a visor, narrows my regard,
And drinking studiously until my thought
Is a blind lowered almost to the sill,
I hanker for that place beyond the sparrow
Where the wrench beds in mud, the sun-hat hangs
In densest branches, and the book is drowned.
Ah, you have read my mind. One more, perhaps . . .
A mezzo-litro. Grazie, professore.

SPELLS, CHARMS,
INCANTATIONS

AGAINST UNRULY ANTS

If the ants do not respond to the conjurer's pleas by leaving, he carries out this threat, destroying their houses by pouring a quantity of water onto the anthill and sprinkling the outer edge and circumference with his so venerated piciete ("tobacco").

come now!
Mother Water
what are the ants
doing around?
wipe them out
they don't obey me

are they perhaps
rooted?
you uproot trees
quickly wash them
away to the far-off
dusty plains
are you perhaps rooted?

come now!
Green Spirit
Tobacco
why delay more?

chase them away
close their town

126   FRANCISCO X. ALARCÓN (1954–2016)
TRANSLATED BY DAVID BOWLES and
XÁNATH CARAZA

CHARM FOR A SWARM OF BEES

When the bees begin to stir, scoop up some earth
With your right hand, sling it under your right foot,
and say:

> Here where I stand I will stake my claim.
> Listen to the land speak, lord of us all:
> Mightier than malice, mightier than spite,
> The master of every man's mother tongue.

When the bees begin to swarm, sift some sand in your
palm,
Scatter it over them like a soft cloud, and say:

> Stay put on this plot, proud sisters in arms!
> Never turn wild and take to the woods.
> What is good for you is good for me,
> As any man will tell you who tends the land.

ANONYMOUS 127
TRANSLATED FROM OLD ENGLISH BY DAVID BARBER

THE NIGHT IS DARKENING ROUND ME

The night is darkening round me
The wild winds coldly blow
But a tyrant spell has bound me
And I cannot cannot go

The giant trees are bending
Their bare boughs weighed with snow
And the storm is fast descending
And yet I cannot go

Clouds beyond clouds above me
Wastes beyond wastes below
But nothing drear can move me
I will not cannot go

HOMAGE TO MY HIPS

these hips are big hips
they need space to
move around in.
they don't fit into little
petty places. these hips
are free hips.
they don't like to be held back.
these hips have never been enslaved,
they go where they want to go
they do what they want to do.
these hips are mighty hips.
these hips are magic hips.
i have known them
to put a spell on a man and
spin him like a top!

FIVE INCONSEQUENTIAL CHARMS

CHARM FOR A SILVER SPOON

Spoon, O spoon,
Wrought from thin silver,
Bright as a small moon,
Drollest and most companionable
Of all utensils of the housewife's table,
Be serviceable beside my cup of tea
And by the fire share bread and milk with me.

CHARM ON MAKING A BED

With sheets cool and smooth
I bid you bring rest,

With the fleece of soft blankets
Lap warmly the spirit,

With the quaintness of quilts
Give whimsical dreams.

CHARM FOR RUNNING WATER

Hesitator,
Faltering from pool to pool,
Leaping like a child,
Or a fawn
Among the rocks,
Leaf-dappled,
Wild and sweet,
Turn not from us
Languid with summer.

CHARM FOR THE DISREPUTABLE CROWS

Crow! crow!
Ironic and rusty,
Raucous-voiced, heavy-winged,
Tattered and dusty,
Tramp bird, scamp bird,
I beg you to fly
In grotesque grandeur
Against my sky.

CHARM FOR A JAR

All the flowers of the garden
Fresh from dew and slant of sunlight
Fresh from song and the loam's clinging,
Beg your kindness, foster-mother.

INVOCATION

There is a woman with a bird's nose
&, in each ear, four or seven holes,
   Mother, you, come,

& the father who is a house,

& all the mountains in little towns,
clarinets, violins, girls with yellow dresses, come,
Chicago, jump the country, come,
Jazzy & your crooked teeth, Lupita.

Come orange blossoms & news,
good luck, juke box, come photobooths,
freight trains.

Come,
   Abraham
   Hannah
   Zewdit
   Tadesse
   Tiny
   Cisco
   Granddaddy, come,
& all the roots of trees & flowers,
street corners & mango stands,

piragua man, come,
silver tooth, back rooms, 12 o'clock,
come cloves & beans & frankincense,
baseball diamond, the dirt track, come Pharoah
& Mary & Nascimento's band,
come beds, whole lakes & keeping time,
come holy ghost & silver fish,
come
    bird,
    bird,
    bird,
& ballet shoes in the church's basement,
come candle & maroon,
cilantro, green, come braid & fist of afro-pick,
come tender head & honey hive,
quick knife, domino, come bomba, come,
fish hook, Inglewood, March, old moon,
come busted piano, ivory key,
come, cousin, come alive,
come, time,
uprock, beach crab, cliff,
come glass eye, nazela, sails,
brother, sisters,
come magnum locks & world of things, sphinx,
desert bottles, indigo, maps,
Sojourner, Lolita, Albizú come,
Gwendolyn, Victor & Lorraine, come Neptune,

Hector Lavoe, Haragu, come,
Adisogdo, come free,
come hips, come foot, come rattlesnake, Jupiter, love
    come,
cardamom & reeds, come wild,
spells, lightning, frogs & rain,
come loss, come teeth, come crows & kites,
conga, conga, & kettle drums,
come holy, holy parade of dirt, come
mis muertos who dance in procession
while tubas play, come.

& a god who is a girl, marigolds
in her hair, see her blow,
into my mouth, a wind of copal
that is smoking, smoking.
& on it, come, ride
into it, come, family,

& ride through the rooms of my house. Into
my veins & brain, come,
the lace of nerves – oh, how
you make
me heaven.

INCANTATION

Give me words to please my tongue
And words in futile strands
Like colored beads, to twine among
The shadows in my hands.

Give me words like instruments
Of steel, to probe my mind,
That I may name its impotence
The small dark of the blind.

Give me words at night to calm
Like herbs; these I shall keep
Pressed to the cheek hot on my palm
To thinly scent my sleep.

INCANTATION

Beginning with a couplet from Carmina Gadelica
and with grace notes from the same source.

I have a charm for the bruising
a charm for the blackening
a charm for cheats and impostors.

I summon from the cold clear air
from the bare branches of the trees
from worms coiling under the ground –

charm against cruel intent
charm for neglect
charm against wicked indifference:

may it lie on the white backs of the breakers of the sea
may it lie on the furthest reaches of the wind.

A salve for those who would grudge against the poor
a salve for those who would harry the innocent
a salve for those who would murder children.

may it lie in the stoniest stretches of the hills
may it lie in the darkest shelving along the shore.

A salve for those that would cram
whatever life they have with possession –
for the rage of owning without entitlement
for the desperate murderous possession of things:

may it lie on the cloud-banks that range across
    the sky
may it lie on the face of Rannoch Moor in its
    remoteness.

A charm against mystification by doctors
a charm against deception by the self-appointed
a charm against horrific insistence:

from the breeze that stirs the last of the yellowing
    leaves
from the slanting of the sun as it falls though the
    window.

A salve against grasping
a salve against preaching
a salve against promises exacted by threat.

Grace of form
grace of voice
grace of virtue
grace of sea

grace of land and air
grace of music
grace of dancing.

A salve against the uselessness of envy
a salve against denial of our own best nature
a salve against bitter enmity and silence

Grace of beauty
grace of spirit
grace of laughter
grace of the fullness of life itself.

A salve to bind us
a salve to strengthen heart and happiness:

may it lie in the star-blanket there to spread over us
may it lie in the first light at the waking of day.

ALEXANDER HUTCHISON (1943—2015)

A CURE FOR PLAGUE

Clap the air, ring bells, fire
your muskets and cannons.
Kill all swallows, flying or nesting.
Coat the doors and window frames
with perfumes and scented oils.
Smoke tobacco from a Dutch pipe.
Apply the entrails of a young pigeon
to your forehead. Wear arsenic in a locket,
or write the word *arsenicum*
on a piece of parchment, hang it
around your neck. Place a pig at the foot
of your bed, sun-dried toads
over your boils. Open the boils,
and with burning herbs – lavender
and feverfew – blister your thighs.
Rub your tongue
with wild beeswax. Sing
into the wound.

THE PEDLAR OF SPELLS

An old man selling charms in a cranny of the town-
wall.
He writes out spells to bless the silk-worms and spells
to protect the corn.

With the money he gets each day he only buys wine;
Nor does he worry when his legs wobble,
For he has a boy to lean on.

THE CURE FOR WARTS

Had I been the seventh son of a seventh son
Living at the dead centre of a wood
Or at the dead end of a lane,
I might have cured by my touch alone
That pair of warts nippling your throat,

Who had no faith in a snail rubbed on your skin
And spiked on a thorn like a king's head,
In my spittle on shrunken stone,
In bathing yourself at the break of dawn
In dew or the black cock's or the bull's blood,

In other such secrets told by way of a sign
Of the existence of one or other god,
So I doubt if any woman's son
Could have cured by his touch alone
That pair of warts nibbling your throat.

SPELL FOR PROTECTING THE HEART
AFTER DEATH

My heart, my mother heart,
Heart of my living on earth.

Spirits, don't grab this heart with your fingers,
Don't steal and crush my heart.
It belongs to the living who walk about in the city.

When I was a child my heart shone in its egg,
My grown heart rose like a heron, cackled like a
     goose, my aged heart
Lay under the back-bent sky; was a dark stone in the
     sky's belt.

This heart belongs to the living who talk and make
     love in the city.

I kneel before a god who holds his tail in his hand.
Friends in the city, make a green scarab; place it over
     my heart,

Let my legs which are tied together be opened;
Let the chief of the gods spread his jaws for me, let the
     doors of Heaven be rolled ajar,
And my heart remain,
This heart that I have from my body.

DIANA O'HEHIR (1922–2021)   143

SPELL SPOKEN BY SUPPLIANT TO HELIOS FOR PROTECTION
from *The Greek Magical Papyri*

This is the charm that will protect you, the charm
That you must wear: Onto lime wood write
With vermilion the secret name, name of
The fifty magic letters. Then say the words:
"Guard me from every daimon of the air,
On the earth and under the earth, guard me
From every angel and phantom, every
Ghostly visitation and enchantment,
Me, your suppliant." Enclose it in a skin
Dyed purple, hang it round your neck and wear it.

INCANTATION

I write your name
   on a sheet
of paper.
   I fold it
in half.

   In the center
of a bowl:
   Lavender.
Quartz.
   A feather.

With a kitchen knife
   I summon blood
to the surface
   of my left palm.
Love line.

   Life line.
Tell me
   what this means.
I clench my fist.
   I squeeze

a drop of ichor
　　over the dead
flowers,
　　the rock and plume.
I strike a match.

　　To vanquish
you from me
　　forever,
I whisper
　　into the pyre.

Good-bye.
　　I bury
your ash
　　in the garden.
Good-bye.

　　Winter
to spring.
　　Good-bye.
Then summer.
　　Nothing blooms

where I keep you.
    Not hoa lan
or birds of paradise
    choking
the encroaching fern.

Except me,
    you still kill
everything.

THE DARK ARTS

BLUE MOTH, BLACK MAGIC

Clorinda was the lady's name.
New Orleans was the town.
A Creole girl of snow and flame,
May dread her master's frown;
Till the blue moth, the live moth,
She stitches to her gown.

Carnations in December's glooms.
Then pistols cocked to kill.
No bullet daunts the Voo-doo doll
That does the lady's will;
While the blue moth, the blue moth,
Flies though its wings are still.

"The Dueling Oaks at dawn, sweetheart,
And quiet for my clay,
Till I remember Jack, the doll,
In the deep grave where I lay.
And Clorinda, Clorinda,
On Earth she shall not stay."

At midnight from the grave he came
Her master cruel and proud.
Clorinda was that lady's name,
But speak it not aloud

In New Orleans where lightnings flame
'Neath Voo-doo's thunder cloud,
And the blue moth, the blue moth,
Floats over beauty's shroud.

A SPELL TO DESTROY LIFE

Listen!
> Now I have come to step over your soul
>> (I know your clan)
>> (I know your name)
>> (I have stolen your spit and buried it under
>> earth)

I bury your soul under earth

I cover you over with black rock

I cover you over with black cloth

I cover you over with black slabs

You disappear forever

Your path leads to the
> Black Coffin
> in the hills of the
>> Darkening Land

So let it be for you

The clay of the hills covers you
The black clay of the Darkening Land

Your soul fades away

It becomes blue (color of despair)

When darkness comes your spirit shrivels and
    dwindles
                  to disappear forever

Listen!

CHERRY
from *Fruit Études*

Her grandmother says Cherry is sweet and kind
If you ruin her, I'll come to your house
Drag you out by your ear
Take a hard branch
Off your crooked ancestry tree and beat you blind

And when I'm dead, I'll haunt you
Curse you
Throw magic spells
Turn you into a hapless
Gonadless monkey
Just for thrills

THE JUGGLERS

A juggler long through all the town
Had rais'd his fortune and renown;
You'd think (so far his art transcends)
The devil at his fingers' ends.

Vice heard his fame, she read his bill;
Convinc'd of his inferior skill,
She sought his booth, and from the croud
Defy'd the man of art aloud.

Is this then he so fam'd for slight,
Can this slow bungler cheat your sight,
Dares he with me dispute the prize?
I leave it to impartial eyes.

Provok'd, the juggler cry'd, 'tis done.
In science I submit to none.

Thus said. The cups and balls he play'd;
By turns, this here, that there, convey'd:
The cards, obedient to his words,
Are by a fillip turn'd to birds;
His little boxes change the grain,
Trick after trick deludes the train.
He shakes his bag, he shows all fair,

His fingers spread, and nothing there,
Then bids it rain with showers of gold,
And now his iv'ry eggs are told,
But when from thence the hen he draws,
Amaz'd spectators humm applause.

Vice now stept forth and took the place,
With all the forms of his grimace.

This magick looking-glass, she cries,
(There, hand it round) will charm your eyes:
Each eager eye the sight desir'd,
And ev'ry man himself admir'd.

Next, to a senator addressing;
See this *Bank-note*; observe the blessing:
Breathe on the bill. Heigh, pass! 'Tis gone.
Upon his lips a padlock shone.
A second puff the magick broke,
The padlock vanish'd, and he spoke.

Twelve bottles rang'd upon the board,
All full, with heady liquor stor'd,
By clean conveyance disappear,
And now two bloody swords are there.

A purse she to a thief expos'd;
At once his ready fingers clos'd:
He opes his fist, the treasure's fled,
He sees a halter in its stead.

She bids Ambition hold a wand,
He grasps a hatchet in his hand.

A box of charity she shows:
Blow here; and a church-warden blows,
'Tis vanish'd with conveyance neat,
And on the table smoaks a treat.

She shakes the dice, the board she knocks,
And from all pockets fills her box.

She next a meagre rake addrest;
This picture see; her shape, her breast!
What youth, and what inviting eyes!
Hold her, and have her. With surprise,
His hand expos'd a box of pills;
And a loud laugh proclaim'd his ills.

A counter, in a miser's hand,
Grew twenty guineas at command;
She bids his heir the summ retain,
And 'tis a counter now again.

A guinea with her touch you see
Take ev'ry shape but Charity;
And not one thing, you saw, or drew,
But chang'd from what was first in view.

The juggler now, in grief of heart,
With this submission own'd her art.
Can I such matchless slight withstand?
How practice hath improv'd your hand!
But now and then I cheat the throng;
You ev'ry day, and all day long.

JOHN GAY (1685 – 1732)   159

AGE OF MAGICIANS

A baroque night advances in its clouds,
maps strain loose and are lost, the flash-flood breaks,
the lifting moonflare lights this field a moment,
while death as a skier curves along the snows,
death as an acrobat swings year to year,
turns down to us the big lace of a nurse.
Roads open black, and the magicians come.

The aim of magicians is inward pleasure.
The prophet lives by faith and not by sight,
Being a visionary, he is divided,
or Cain, forever shaken by his crime.
Magnetic ecstasy, a trance of doom
mean the magician, worshipping a darkness
with gongs and lurid guns, the colors of force.
He is against the unity of light.

The Magician has his symbols, brings up his children
        by them:
the march-step, the staircase at night, the long
        cannon.
The children grow in authority and become
Molitor, Dr. Passavant, powerful Dr. Falcon,
bring their professors, and soon may govern
the zone, the zodiac, the king on his throne.

"Because the age holds its own dangers.
Because snow comes with lightnings, omens with all
        seasons."
(The Prophet covers his face against the wall,
weeps, fights to think again, to plan to start
the dragon, the ecliptic, and the heart.)

The Magician lifts himself higher than the world.
The Prophets were more casual. They endured,
and in the passive dread of solitude
heard calls, followed veiled, in midnight humility.

They claimed no preference; they separated
unity from blindness
living from burning
tribute from tribute.

They have gone under, and do they come again?
The index of prophecy is light
and steeped therein
the world with all its signatures visible.

*

Does this life permit its living to wear strength?
Who gives it, protects it. It is food.
Who refuses it, it eats in time as food.
It is the world and it eats the world.

Who knows this, knows. This has been said.
This is the vision in the age of magicians:
it stands at immense barriers, before mountains:
"I came to you in the form of a line of men,
and when you threw down the paper, and when you
        sat at the play,
and when you killed the spider, and when you saw the
        shadow
of the fast plane skim fast over your lover's face.
And when you saw the table of diplomats,
the newsreel of ministers, the paycut slip,
the crushed child's head, clean steel, factories,
the chessmen on the marble of the floor,
each flag a country, each chessman a live man,
one side advancing southward to the pit,
one side advancing northward to the lake,
and when you saw the tree, half bright half burning.
You never enquired into these meanings.
If you had done this, you would have been restored."

The word is war.
And there is a prediction that you are the avenger.

They cut the people's hands, and their shoulders were
        left,
they cut their feet off, and their thighs were whole,

they cut them down to the torso, but the voice
    shouted,
they cut the head off, but the heart rang out.

And in the residential districts, where nothing ever
    happens,
armies of magicians filled the streets,
shouting
Need! Bread! Blood! Death!

And all this is because of you.
And all this is avenged by you.
Your index light, your voice the voice,
your tree half green and half burning,
half dead half bright,
your cairns, your beacons, your tree in green and
    flames,
unbending smoke in the sky, planes, noise, the
    darkness,
magic to fight. Much to restore, now know. Now be
Seer son of Sight, Hearer, of Ear, at last.

NINE WITCHES

i.

The raven I had tucked beneath my arm,
He scritched and scritched. I took his head in hand
And broke the voice off with a little twist.
I have the beak, the tongue; one curving wing
To fan the fire, raise a breeze, or shade the eyes
If the moon glares white hot and the sparking stars.

ii.

I've been among the mammals gathering off
The rabid wolf's chin slather; a doe's scut, bristles
From a fox's cheek, the raisins rabbits drop
Up on the hillside. Asleep in the gorse and thorn I
    found
Your fool cat Scruple, her belly full of mouse and
    shrew.
Here she is, sharp and scowling in the burlap sack.

iii.

I lay along the furrow where wheat is newly sown.
I heard thaw in the soil, the earthworms moving,
    moles

Waking in their dark tunnels, mending their ways.
It was dark with heavy water, zero stars.
From my throat I gargled out the mildew spell.
My shoes and cloak and fists are full of wheat seed.

iv.

I have been to the Euphrates gathering skulls
Quite fresh, the faces on them, the wide eyes
Still full of tears. I gathered them in public highways,
Back gardens, mosques, cars, ditches, hospitals.
Three dozen here are threaded on barbed wire,
All I could drag back. I'll get more in tomorrow.

v.

It was so cool all day beneath the cradle.
I almost slept the baby's sleep; when the night was
        still
I sucked her breath, I breathed her breathing in,
So fresh it was, and sweet, I held it close
Until her fitful body like the night outside
Fell calm. I held it till I got back here.

vi.

I had a knife when I went down the mountain.
I marked my destination with a cross.
I found Avila: the woman bent in prayer,
Teresa, Saint: *to pray is labour, making prayer*
A holy act like stirring soup, or weaving, sweeping.
I slit her weaving, diced her prayer, I swept her up.

vii.

The murderer was dangling from his noose, out
On the high road by the gibbet (the watchman
        snored).
Veins watered him a week ago, run dry now.
He sagged, was sallow, peck marks in his eyes.
I stole the shirt and let the ribs show through,
The trousers and the shoes, left him forked and
        human.

viii.

The screech owl laid nine eggs in my pointed hat,
Bedding them with black down from her breast and
        tail.
She stayed with them until the moon went up:
She climbed the steep sky with it, screaming, circling.

I took my stinking hat and flew for home
Faster than bird of prey. A soufflé, sisters?

ix.

The latest, the new, the novice witch am I.
I went abroad tonight for apprentice things,
Poppies, hemlock, hen-bane, libbards-bane,
Wild fig from graves, snails, toads and sarin, roaches.
I did not intend to find peach, pear or apple
Or the god of love perched in a loquat laughing.

I stole his bow, his blindfold, his winged shoes;
I took his laughter and I left him there
Stricken on his bough, eyes vacant, stopped
As a clockwork bird run down, as a toy outgrown,
Or a child who dreamt he was free but woke up stone.
I share out the laugh with my sisters. We jig on the
    heath.

VOODOO II: MONEY

If magick brings it, it will be tainted, damp, ill-hued,
the wrong patriot will grimace from its center,
denominations will mean nothing. Money that passes
through hands blackened with the powder of ill wish,
hands spiced with incantation oils,
won't ever spend well. It will appear green and viable
only for a second, a second just wide enough
to turn you into a certified fool – then, as you hold
it in front of you like a shield against weather,
you will know. It's too thin to hold tomorrow back.

HOUSEHOLD MAGIC

MY FATHER

The memory of my father is wrapped in white paper
like slices of bread for the workday.

Like a magician pulling out rabbits and towers from
    his hat,
he pulled out from his little body – love.

The rivers of his hands
poured into his good deeds.

THE MAGICIAN'S DAUGHTER

My father was always the magician,
not I. One swift pull and
the silk streamers would spill
from his mouth, flooding the floor.
The chains always broke. The cage always
vanished. The canary always returned,
chirping, from the dead.

At nineteen the magic came calling.
At the paintball park I swallowed a bullet
and spat it out whole. During dinner
the knife fell through my palm,
tumbling into the curry.
Mama soaked the drops up with a dishrag
until it squeaked.

The fifth time after I made my
cabinet escape, Mama turned it into
plywood. Said, this country is no place
for magic. Tricks do not fill empty bowls
with rice, only rabbits. Said, you are not
Houdini. You will not come back
alive.

But the pennies keep turning up
under my tongue. Everything I eat
tastes like rust. My skin won't stop
humming. All my rings have turned
into links. Gingerly, I pluck the coins out
and coax them into tiny molten suns.
They flood the floor with light.

NOTHING I CAN LOSE

When I left my father's house
the sun was halfway up,
my father held it to my chin
like a buttercup.

My father was a snake-oil man
a wizard, trickster, liar,
but this was his best trick,
we kissed goodbye in fire.

A mile above Niagara Falls
a dove gave me the news
of his death. I didn't miss a step,
there's nothing I can lose.

Tomorrow I'll invent a trick
I do not know tonight,
the wind, the pole will tell me what
and the friendly blinding light.

ELEGY FOR A MAGICIAN

Once I got so skinny
that I turned pale blue
in places and became ethereal
against the hard knocks
of the broken furniture
in the depression years,
but when my mother screamed
at me through one ear
to come and eat my beans,
the other ear stayed fixed
to the dying radio while
Chandu the Magician hissed
and whispered me away
inside his crackling box,
up the aerial and out
into the open airways as
the blue genie of Brooklyn.

LUCK

My mother threw pinches of spilt salt
over her left shoulder, would toss water
that had boiled eggs onto the garden;
crossed knives were swiftly uncrossed on the table.
For good luck: her youngest brother's signet ring,
its horseshoe worn smooth; the rabbit's foot
that was her mother's; a shamrock, four-leaved,
pressed inside her unused missal.

By small margins, sometimes, we find our way
or lose it. If charms that kiss the hem
of a frowning god, can help, let's have them.
Secure all mirrors, slip on the horseshoe ring
and then, with a pinch of salt, plant seeds where
the egg-water fell. Tend what grows there.

176   DIANE FAHEY (1945−)

PRESTO!

The magician placed a rabbit inside the red box
and with the wave of the wand *presto!* it went
up in smoke, now a stunned dove on stage.
He waved once more and *presto!* another blast
of smoke, another dove. The birds became exotic

even though Abuela kept a palomar in the back
of the house, the ground snowy with down
but so stinky Abuela called them turds with feathers.
How she missed her birds, the way I missed
Mexico and every word that sounded Mexican

tugged at my heart. *Presto!* the magician yelled
and I wanted to switch places with the doves
that must have come from Abuela's palomar
in Michoacán. I had been inside the cage
to clean it out so many times while Abuela

pleaded with me to be careful in case an egg
had fallen from its nest. "Let's put it back,"
she suggested whenever I found one, and I wanted
to be put back the same way, into that palomar
where the doves sang *cucurrucucú, cucurrucucú.*

And the smell wouldn't bother me anymore
because I would be home again. Oh, magic man,
presto! presto! presto! everything back to Spanish –
dove to paloma, house to casa, Abuela to happy lady
caressing her birds in the glorious Mexican afternoons.

ABRACADABRA

Art Is All was the family motto
Bidden in a childhood tucked
Right inside a gloomy wood.
Almost annihilated, we tried to
Cultivate care, keep ourselves
Alive as the Art that was,
Dare I say, really *Father*.
All to keep spirits up, we daughters,
Brave little sorceresses, we
Revelled in contradicting with
Artful spells – our cunning bailiwick.

THE ALCHEMISTS

By day
they bent over lead's
heavy spirit of illness,
asking it to be gold,
the lord from humble beginnings.

And the mad soul of mercury
fell through their hands
through settled floors
and came to rest
silver and deadly
in a hidden corner
where it would grow.

Gold was the property
that could take sickness out
from lead.
It was fire
held still.
At night
they lifted the glass
of black grapes
and sugar to their lips
and drank the flaked gold
suspended in wine

like sparks of fire,
then watched it fall
like fool's gold
to the bottom of a pond.

Yesterday, my father behind a curtain
in the sick ward
heard a doctor
tell a man where the knife
would cut flesh.
Listen, my father said,
that man is saying a poem.
No, he's telling a story.
No, I believe
he is reading from a magical book.

But he was only a man
talking to iron,
willing it to be gold.

If it had worked
we would kneel down before it
and live forever,
all base metals
in ceremonial fire.

LINDA HOGAN (1947–)   181

ABRACADABRA

My mother holds the wriggling mouse
in her gloved hand
thumb poised above its vertebrae

My father in his white coat behind her
whispers the right places to break

She shakes her head – *No, no*

Mercy is the small name
we give an animal not ourselves

I knew she had it in her, my mother
holding me all those years ago
in the chair as my father cut my hair –

So you don't look like a girl

Against the back of my skull
he made a fist & pulled

Like a magician & his assistant
they did the act together – Transformation
Dismemberment & Shove Her in a Hat!

The girl vanished under the black scrim
& a boy was lifted by the neck

That cowlick –
it was the only thing wild about me

In my twenties I grew my hair out
& slathered perm salt to break
the disulfide bonds

I stroked my curls, each strand
a helix hissing secrets

I thought if I looked foreign enough
no one could claim me

not even shame
which, as all things
must grow from the root

INDIAN ROPE TRICK

It's the mystery's favorite trick: weaving
the intricate rope of someone's life, then
lifting it for them to climb and somewhere
near the top . . . disappear.

Two weeks ago my brother told me
he'd shot nine holes. Pain was lousy, he said,
but went on to try out punchlines he'd been
practicing for his meeting with the Maker.

I'm not afraid to die, he said
with that curious wonder he had
since the diagnosis. But this time
he added he had no regrets.
None worth counting, anyway.

I'd taken my phone on my walk and was talking
to him from the mountain, at the level of ravens
and hawks. He'd had a wonderful life, he said,
which caused the rope of it to rise and grow taut
so we could see it in all its color: There in his yellow

cowboy pajamas with his champion Alaskan yoyo.
There in the glow of his cherry-bomb days.

There at the helm of the stolen tractor on a joyride
over the golf club greens. And look: now he's doing

figure eights on his forklift in the basement of Kodak.
Now he's blasting off, bottle-rocket-style, to
international VP. See him there in Paris and Philly?
See him adrift on South Carolina's inlet seas?

Here come the whole buzzing swarm
of friends drawn in by the honey of his ease.
Ah . . . we seem to have followed that rope
right up through the clouds.

I couldn't have asked for more, he said.
And his exhale filled the valley
so the hawks lifted up on the rising air.
And we said goodbye.

MY FATHER IS A RETIRED MAGICIAN
for ifa, p.t. & bisa

my father was a retired magician
which accounts for my irregular behavior
everythin comes outta magic hats
or bottles wit no bottoms & parakeets
are as easy to get as a couple a rabbits
or 3 fifty cent pieces/ 1958

my daddy retired from magic & took
up another trade cuz this friend of mine
from the 3rd grade asked to be made white
on the spot

what cd any self-respectin colored american magician
do wit such an outlandish request/ cept
put all them razzamatazz hocus pocus zippity-do-dah
thingamajigs away   cuz
colored chirren believin in magic
waz becomin politically dangerous for the race
& waznt nobody gonna be made white
on the spot   just
from a clap of my daddy's hands

& the reason i'm so peculiar's
cuz i been studyin up on my daddy's technique

186

& everythin i do is magic these days
& it's very colored
very now you see it/ now you
dont mess wit me
                i come from a family of retired
sorcerers/ active houngans & pennyante fortune
    tellers
wit 41 million spirits critturs & celestial bodies
on our side
        i'll listen to yr problems
        help wit yr career   yr lover   yr wanderin
            spouse
        make yr grandma's stay in heaven more
            gratifyin
        ease yr mother thru menopause & show yr
            son
        how to clean his room

YES YES YES   3 wishes is all you get
    scarlet ribbons for yr hair
        benwa balls via hong kong
            a miniature of machu picchu

all things are possible
but aint no colored magician in her right mind
gonna make you   white
    i mean

this is blk magic
you lookin at
    & i'm fixin you up good n colored
& you gonna be colored all yr life
& you gonna love it/ bein colored/ all yr life/ colored
    & love it
love it/ bein colored/

LOVE MAGIC

THE INNOCENT MAGICIAN; OR,
A CHARM AGAINST LOVE

A Great, but Harmless Conjurer am I,
That can Love's Captives set at Liberty;
Hearts led astray by his deluding Flame,
I to their peaceful Dwellings can reclaim;
Love's Wings I clip, and take from him his Arms,
By the sole Virtue of my Sacred Charms;

His Empire shakes when I appear in Sight,
My Words the Wing'd and Quiver'd Boys affright;
Their close Retreats my boundless Power invades,
Nor can they hide them in their Myrtle Shades.
Their Sun's bright Rays, they now eclips'd shall find,
Whose fancy'd Light strikes giddy Lovers blind,

Rays of fair Eyes, which they proclaim Divine,
And boast they can *Sol*'s dazling Beams out-shine.
The Storms of Sighs, and Rivers of their Eyes,
My Skill allays, and their large Current dryes.
Hearts that are dead, I from their Graves retrieve,
And by my Magick-Spell can make them live.

For know, they're only Tricks, and subtil Arts,
With which the Tyrant Love ensnares our Hearts;
This Traytor plants his Toils to gain his Prize,

In Curls of Flaxen Hair, and Sparkling Eyes:
In each soft Look, and Smile, he sets a Gin,
White Hands, or Snowy Breasts can tempt us in.

Wholly on Mischief is his Mind employ'd,
His fairest Shows do greatest Dangers hide;
With Charming Sounds his Vot'ryes he beguiles,
Till he destroys them by his *Syren*'s Wiles;
His Cunning *Circes* ev'ry where deceive,
And Men of Souls and Humane Shape bereave.

A thousand other Arts this Treach'rous Boy,
To heedless Lovers Ruine does employ.
Be watchful then, and his Allurements shun,
So ends my Charm. Run to your Freedom, Run.

SYMPATHETIC MAGIC

In southern Germany, as late as the nineteenth century, in order to increase the fertility of the soil, the peasant used to take his wife to the fields and have intercourse with her in a furrow. This is called sympathetic magic.

C. G. Jung

The corn is planted, the wheat is planted,
and – our best nights of love long gone –
I take your hand and lead you to the fields.
Cicadas, crickets, and locusts rub their legs together.
Fireflies cling to their lamps like Nepalese guides.
Our children sleep in the house, dreaming of harvests.

Imagining melons, I place my hands under your
buttocks, set you into the furrow like a baker
taking fresh bread from his oven. The soil
is cracked and dry, only a hint of weeds rising.
I lower myself beside you, purposeful as a king
without heirs. And then I rise to you, sweet
and ambitious as the first rains of April.

I think, again, of our first nights of love,
your body a trellis beneath me, your lips
mangos on a parched tongue. And as we sway
together, resurrected, in our barren fields

I feel the corn, the wheat, the widening soil
rise to the light of your shuddering body.

CIRCE

It was easy enough
to bend them to my wish,
it was easy enough
to alter them with a touch,
but you
adrift on the great sea,
how shall I call you back?

Cedar and white ash,
rock-cedar and sand plants
and tamarisk
red cedar and white cedar
and black cedar from the inmost forest,
fragrance upon fragrance
and all of my sea-magic is for nought.

It was easy enough —
a thought called them
from the sharp edges of the earth;
they prayed for a touch,
they cried for the sight of my face,
they entreated me
till in pity
I turned each to his own self.

Panther and panther,
then a black leopard
follows close –
black panther and red
and a great hound,
a god-like beast,
cut the sand in a clear ring
and shut me from the earth,
and cover the sea-sound
with their throats,
and the sea-roar with their own barks
and bellowing and snarls,
and the sea-stars
and the swirl of the sand,
and the rock-tamarisk
and the wind resonance –
but not your voice.

It is easy enough to call men
from the edges of the earth,
It is easy enough to summon them to my feet
with a thought –
it is beautiful to see the tall panther
and the sleek deer-hounds
circle in the dark.
It is easy enough
to make cedar and white ash fumes

into palaces
and to cover the sea-caves
with ivory and onyx.

But I would give up
rock-fringes of coral
and the inmost chamber
of my island palace
and my own gifts
and the whole region
of my power and magic
for your glance.

THE BALLAD OF THE ENAMORD MAGE

How the Earth turns round under the Sun I know,
And how the Numbers in the Constellations glow,
How all Forms in Time will grow
And return to their single Source
Informd by Grief, Joy, insatiable Desire
And cold Remorse.

Serpents I have seen bend the Evening Air
Where Flowers that once Men and Women were
Voiceless spread their innocent Lustre.
I have seen green Globes of Water
Enter the Fire. In my Sight
Tears have drownd the Flames of Animal Delight.

I, a poor writer, who knows not
where or wherefor my body was begot.

In a World near a City in a green Tree
I was once a Bird shot down by Thee.
And Thou, Beloved, shot from Thy young Bow
An Arrow from which my Blood doth daily flow
And stoppd the Song
That now I sing Thee all Night long.

I, turning my verse, waiting for the rime,
that know not the meaning of my name.

In a place where a Stone was, hot in the Sun,
I was once a Mage, dry as a Bone,
And calld to me a Demon of myself alone
Who from my Thirst conjured a green River
And out of my Knowledge I saw Thee run,
A Spring of pure Water.

I, late at night, facing the page
writing my fancies in a literal age.

How all beings into all beings pass,
How the great Beasts eat the human Grass,
And the Faces of Men in the World's Glass
Are faces of Apes, Birds, Diamonds,
Worlds and insubstantial Shapes
Conjured out of the Dust – Alas!
These things I know.
Worlds out of Worlds in Magic grow.

I, mortal, that live by chance,
and know not why you love,
praise the great wheel where the spirits dance,
for by your side I move.

LOVE AND BLACK MAGIC

To the woods, to the woods is the wizard gone;
In his grotto the maiden sits alone.
She gazes up with a weary smile
At the rafter-hanging crocodile,
The slowly swinging crocodile.
Scorn has she of her master's gear,
Cauldron, alembic, crystal sphere,
Phial, philtre – "Fiddlededee
For all such trumpery trash!" quo' she.
"A soldier is the lad for me;
Hey and hither, my lad!

"Oh, here have I ever lain forlorn:
My father died ere I was born,
Mother was by a wizard wed,
And oft I wish I had died instead –
Often I wish I were long time dead.
But, delving deep in my master's lore,
I have won of magic power such store
I can turn a skull – oh, fiddlededee
For all this curious craft!" quo' she.
"A soldier is the lad for me;
Hey and hither, my lad!

"To bring my brave boy unto my arms.
What need have I of magic charms –
'Abracadabra!' and 'Prestopuff'?
I have but to wish, and that is enough.
The charms are vain, one wish is enough.
My master pledged my hand to a wizard;
Transformed would I be to toad or lizard
If e'er he guessed – but fiddlededee
For a black-browed sorcerer, now," quo' she.
"Let Cupid smile and the fiend must flee;
Hey and hither, my lad."

NECROMANCER

the dreads
of the dreaded boy
shake to his hum
move like serpents
charming prey
as he dances
in front of me
brewing some potion
sautéing garlic
and ganja in air
I'm bewitched
by the swaying of his hair
his yellow gold yellow
in the dying sun
and the spellbound prey
the man he has won
by singing and conjuring
as day comes undone

LOVE SPELL

"Love spell of attraction over myrrh ... while offering it over coals, recite the spell."
    — from *The Greek Magical Papyri,*
        edited by Hanz Dieter Betz

If he should eat, keep him from eating.
If he should look, stop him from looking.
If he should sleep, make him unable
to sleep with any other.

And do not enter through his eyes
or through his nails, or even through his navel,
but through his breath, burning his lungs, his chest,
his heart, his liver, his bones and his marrow.

As you burn in this fire, so burn the brain
of the one I love. Turn his intestines
inside out, suck out his blood drop by drop
until he comes to me.

Match palm to palm and fasten mouth to mouth.
Press elbow to elbow. Keep thigh
close to thigh. Fit dark to dark.
Join him to me. Now. Always.

ELISE PASCHEN (1959—)   203

BLACK MAGIC

magic
      my man
is you
      turning
my body into
a thousand

smiles.
      black
magic is your
touch
      making
me breathe.

THE LOST MAGIC

White in her snowy stone, and cold,
    With azure veins and shining arms,
Pygmalion doth his bride behold,
    Rapt on her pure and sculptured charms.

Ah! in those half-divine old days
    Love still worked miracles for men;
The gods taught lovers wondrous ways
    To breathe a soul in marble then.

He gazed, he yearned, he vowed, he wept.
    Some secret witchery touched her breast;
And, laughing April tears, she stepped
    Down to his arms and lay at rest.

Dear artist of the storied land!
    I too have loved a heart of stone.
What was thy charm of voice or hand,
    Thy secret spell, Pygmalion?

AFTER LOVE

There is no magic any more,
  We meet as other people do,
You work no miracle for me
  Nor I for you.

You were the wind and I the sea —
  There is no splendor any more,
I have grown listless as the pool
  Beside the shore.

But though the pool is safe from storm
  And from the tide has found surcease,
It grows more bitter than the sea,
  For all its peace.

206   SARA TEASDALE (1884—1933)

THE POET AS
MAGICIAN

BROWNING RESOLVES TO BE A POET

In these red London labyrinths
I find that I have chosen
the most curious of human professions,
though given that all are curious, in their way.
Like alchemists
who looked for the philosopher's stone
in elusive quicksilver,
I shall make ordinary words –
the marked cards of the sharper, the people's coinage –
yield up the magic that was theirs
when Thor was inspiration and eruption,
thunder and worship.
In the wording of the day,
I in my turn will say eternal things;
I will try to be not unworthy
of the great echo of Byron.
This dust that is me will be invulnerable.
If a woman shares my love,
my poem will graze the tenth sphere of the concentric
        heavens;
if a woman shrugs off my love,
I will make music out of my misery,
a vast river reverberating through time.
I will live by forgetting myself.
I will be the face I half-see and forget,

I will be Judas who accepts
the blessed destiny of being a traitor,
I will be Caliban in the swamp,
I will be a mercenary dying
without fear or faith,
I will be Polycrates, horrified to see
the ring returned by destiny,
I will be the friend who hates me.
Persia will grant me the nightingale, Rome the sword.
Agonies, masks, and resurrections
will weave and unweave my fate
and at some point I will be Robert Browning.

"I BROKE THE SPELL THAT HELD ME LONG"

I broke the spell that held me long,
The dear, dear witchery of song.
I said, the poet's idle lore
Shall waste my prime of years no more,
For Poetry, though heavenly born,
Consorts with poverty and scorn.

I broke the spell – nor deemed its power
Could fetter me another hour.
Ah, thoughtless! how could I forget
Its causes were around me yet?
For wheresoe'er I looked, the while,
Was Nature's everlasting smile.

Still came and lingered on my sight
Of flowers and streams the bloom and light,
And glory of the stars and sun; –
And these and poetry are one.
They, ere the world had held me long,
Recalled me to the love of song.

NIGHT MADNESS POEM

There's a poem in my head
like too many cups of coffee.
A pea under twenty eiderdowns.
A sadness in my heart like stone.
A telephone. And always my
night madness that outs like bats
across this Texas sky.

I'm the crazy lady they warned you about.
The she of rumor talked about —
and worse, who talks.

It's no secret.
I'm here. Under a circle of light.
The light always on, resisting a glass,
an easy cigar. The kind

who reels the twilight sky.
Swoop circling.
I'm witch woman high
on tobacco and holy water.

I'm a woman delighted with her disasters.
They give me something to do.
A profession of sorts.

Keeps me industrious
and of some serviceable use.

In dreams the origami of the brain
opens like a fist, a pomegranate,
an expensive geometry.

Not true.
I haven't a clue
why I'm rumpled tonight.

Choose your weapon.
Mine – the telephone, my tongue.
Both black as a gun.

I have the magic of words,
the power to charm and kill at will.
To kill myself or to aim haphazardly.
And kill you.

WE ARE THE YOUNG MAGICIANS

Go sit yo ass down
we don't need no volunteers
to disappear
from a box trap door
a hole in the floor
we reappear
folks you never seen before
reach deep
behind black velvet curtains

we don't need no trick cane
to amaze
with a mere wave of the pen
we transform grey concrete
to yellow brick roads

we don't pull no rabbits
from a hat
we pull rainbows
from a trash can
we pull hope
from the dictionary
n teach it how to ride the subway

we don't guess the card in yo hand
we know it
aim to change it
yeah
we know magic
and don't be so sure that card in yo hand
is the Ace

RUTH FORMAN (1968−)   215

SORCERY

there are some people i know
whose beauty
is a crime.
who make you so crazy
you don't know
whether to throw yourself
at them
or kill them.
which makes
for permanent madness.
which could be
bad for you.
you better be on the lookout
for such circumstances.

stay away
from the night.
they most likely lurk
in corners of the room
where they think
they being inconspicuous
but they so beautiful
an aura
gives them away.

stay away
from the day.
they most likely
be walking
down the street
when you least
expect it
trying to look
ordinary
but they so fine

they break your heart
by making you dream
of other possibilities.

stay away
from crazy music.
they most likely
be creating it.
cuz when you're that beautiful
you can't help
putting it out there.
everyone knows
how dangerous
that can get.

stay away
from magic shows.
especially those
involving words.
words are very
tricky things.
everyone knows
words
the most common
instruments of
illusion.

they most likely
be saying them,
breathing poems
so rhythmic
you can't help
but dance.

and once
you start dancing
to words
you might never
stop.

DILIGENCE IS TO MAGIC AS PROGRESS
IS TO FLIGHT

With an elephant to ride upon – "with rings on her
     fingers and bells on her toes,"
  she shall outdistance calamity anywhere she goes.
Speed is not in her mind inseparable from carpets.
     Locomotion arose
  in the shape of an elephant; she clambered up and
    chose
to travel laboriously. So far as magic carpets are
     concerned, she knows
  that although the semblance of speed may attach to
    scarecrows
of aesthetic procedure, the body of it is embodied in
     such of those
  tough-grained animals as have outstripped man's
    whim to suppose
them ephemera, and have earned that fruit of their
     ability to endure blows
  which dubs them prosaic necessities – not curios.

IN MEMORY OF W. H. AUDEN

I am going over my early rages again,
my first laments and ecstasies,
my old indictments and spiritualities.
I am standing, like Schiller, in front of Auden's door
waiting for his carved face to let me in.
In my hand is *The Poem of My Heart* I dragged
from one ruined continent to the other,
all my feelings slipping out on the sidewalk.
It was warm and hopeful in his small cave
waiting for the right word to descend
but it was cold and brutal outside on Fourth Street
as I walked back to the Seventh Avenue subway,
knowing, as I reached the crowded stairway,
that I would have to wait for ten more years
or maybe twenty more years for the first riches
to come my way, and knowing that the stick
of that old Prospero would never rest
on my poor head, dear as he was with his robes
and his books of magic, good and wise as he was
in his wrinkled suit and his battered slippers.
– Oh good and wise, but not enough to comfort me,
so loving was he with his other souls.
I had to wait like clumsy Caliban,
a sucker for every vagueness and degeneration.
I had to find my own way back, I had to

free myself, I had to find my own pleasure
in my own sweet cave, with my own sweet music.
   Once a year, later even once a month,
I stood on the shores of Bleecker and Horatio
waving goodbye to that ship all tight and yare
and that great wizard, bobbing up and down
like a dreaming sailor out there, disappearing
just as he came, only this time his face more weary
and his spirit more grave than when he first arrived
to take us prisoner on our own small island,
that poet I now could talk to, that wrinkled priest
whose neck I'd hang on, that magician
who could release me now, whom I release and
      remember.

from LYRICS: II

First, a poem must be magical,
Then musical as a sea-gull.
It must be a brightness moving
And hold secret a bird's flowering.
It must be slender as a bell,
And it must hold fire as well.
It must have the wisdom of bows
And it must kneel like a rose.
It must be able to hear
The luminance of dove and deer.
It must be able to hide
What it seeks, like a bride.
And over all I would like to hover
God, smiling from the poem's cover.

THE TWO TREES

Beloved, gaze in thine own heart,
The holy tree is growing there;
From joy the holy branches start,
And all the trembling flowers they bear.
The changing colours of its fruit
Have dowered the stars with merry light;
The surety of its hidden root
Has planted quiet in the night;
The shaking of its leafy head
Has given the waves their melody,
And made my lips and music wed,
Murmuring a wizard song for thee.
There the Loves a circle go,
The flaming circle of our days,
Gyring, spiring to and fro
In those great ignorant leafy ways;
Remembering all that shaken hair
And how the wingèd sandals dart,
Thine eyes grow full of tender care:
Beloved, gaze in thine own heart.

Gaze no more in the bitter glass
The demons, with their subtle guile,
Lift up before us when they pass,
Or only gaze a little while;

For there a fatal image grows
That the stormy night receives,
Roots half hidden under snows,
Broken boughs and blackened leaves.

FOR KIDS OF
ALL AGES

THE CONJUROR

When I am a man and can do as I wish,
  With no one to ask if I may,
Although I'll play cricket a little and fish,
  I'll conjure the most of each day.

The conjuror's life is so easy and grand;
  He makes such superior jokes –
O, it's splendid to stand with a wand in your hand,
  And puzzle relations and folks.

If eggs should be wanted, you turn to a friend,
  And draw two or three from his hair;
If a rabbit is wished, and his hat he will lend,
  You wave, and behold, one is there!

To pound a gold watch into thousands of bits
  And restore it as good as before
Is a life that beats even a Major's to fits, –
  Apart from the absence of gore.

TWO NURSERY RHYMES

MILKING

Cushy cow, bonny, let down thy milk,
And I will give thee a gown of silk;
A gown of silk and a silver tee,
If thou wilt let down thy milk for me.

CHURNING

Come, butter, come,
Come, butter, come;
Peter stands at the gate
Waiting for a butter cake.
Come, butter, come.

THANKSGIVING MAGIC

Thanksgiving Day I like to see
Our cook perform her witchery.
She turns a pumpkin into pie
As easily as you or I
Can wave a hand or wink an eye.
She takes leftover bread and muffin
And changes them to turkey stuffin'.
She changes cranberries to sauce
And meats to stews and stews to broths;
And when she mixes gingerbread
It turns into a man instead
With frosting collar 'round his throat
And raisin buttons down his coat.
Oh, some like magic made by wands,
   And some read magic out of books,
And some like fairy spells and charms
   But I like magic made by cooks!

ROWENA BASTIN BENNETT (1896–1981)

THE TRUANTS

Ere my heart beats too coldly and faintly
   To remember sad things, yet be gay,
I would sing a brief song of the world's little children
    Magic hath stolen away.

The primroses scattered by April,
   The stars of the wide Milky Way,
Cannot outnumber the hosts of the children
    Magic hath stolen away.

The buttercup green of the meadows,
   The snow of the blossoming may,
Lovelier are not than the legions of children
    Magic hath stolen away.

The waves tossing surf in the moonbeam,
   The albatross lone on the spray,
Alone know the tears wept in vain for the children
    Magic hath stolen away.

In vain: for at hush of the evening,
   When the stars twinkle into the grey,
Seems to echo the far-away calling of children
    Magic hath stolen away.

MR. MISTOFFELEES

You ought to know Mr. Mistoffelees!
The Original Conjuring Cat —
(There can be no doubt about that).
Please listen to me and don't scoff. All his
Inventions are off his own bat.
There's no such Cat in the metropolis;
He holds all the patent monopolies
For performing surprising illusions
And creating eccentric confusions.
  At prestidigitation
    And at legerdemain
  He'll defy examination
    And deceive you again.
The greatest magicians have something to learn
From Mr. Mistoffelees' Conjuring Turn.
Presto!
  Away we go!
    And we all say: OH!
      Well I never!
      Was there ever
      A Cat so clever
        As Magical Mr. Mistoffelees!

He is quiet and small, he is black
From his ears to the tip of his tail;
He can creep through the tiniest crack,
He can walk on the narrowest rail.
He can pick any card from a pack,
He is equally cunning with dice;
He is always deceiving you into believing
That he's only hunting for mice.
    He can play any trick with a cork
        Or a spoon and a bit of fish-paste;
      If you look for a knife or a fork
        And you think it is merely misplaced –
You have seen it one moment, and then it is *gawn*!
But you'll find it next week lying out on the lawn.
    And we all say: OH!
      Well I never!
      Was there ever
      A Cat so clever
        As Magical Mr. Mistoffelees!

His manner is vague and aloof,
You would think there was nobody shyer –
But his voice has been heard on the roof
When he was curled up by the fire.
And he's sometimes been heard by the fire
When he was about on the roof –
(At least we all *heard* that somebody purred)

Which is incontestable proof
   Of his singular magical powers:
      And I have known the family to call
   Him in from the garden for hours,
      While he was asleep in the hall.
And not long ago this phenomenal Cat
Produced seven *kittens* right out of a hat!
   And we all said: OH!
      Well I never!
      Did you ever
      Know a Cat so clever
         As Magical Mr. Mistoffelees!

T. S. ELIOT (1888—1965)

A LOVE STORY

He was a Wizard's son,
    She an Enchanter's daughter;
He dabbled in Spells for fun,
    Her father some magic had taught her.

They loved – but alas! to agree
    Their parents they couldn't persuade.
An Enchanter and Wizard, you see,
    Were natural rivals in trade –
And the market for magic was poor –
    There was scarce enough business for two
So what started rivalry pure
    Into hatred and jealousy grew.

Now the lovers were dreadfully good;
    But when there was really no hope,
After waiting as long as they could,
    What else could they do but elope?
They eloped in a hired coupé;
    And the youth, with what magic he knew –
Made it go fully five miles a day.
    (Such wonders can sorcery do!)

Then the maiden her witcheries plied,
    And enchanted the cabman so much,

When they got to the end of their ride
    Not a cent of his fare would he touch!
Now they're married and live to this day
    In a nice little tower, alone,
For the building of which, by the way,
    Their parents provided the stone.

Then the parents relented? Oh, no!
    They pursued with the fury of brutes,
But arrived just too late for the show,
    Through a leak in their seven-league boots;
And finding their children were wed,
    Into such a wild rage they were thrown,
They rushed on each other instead
    And each turned the other to stone.

Then the lovers, since lumber was high,
    And bricks were as then quite unknown,
As soon as their tears were quite dry –
    They quarried their parents for stone.

And now in a nice little tower,
    In Blissfulness tinged with Remorse,
They live like as not to this hour –
    (Unless they have got a divorce).

Crime, Wickedness, Villainy, Vice,
   And sin only misery bring;
If you want to be Happy and Nice,
   Be good and all that sort of thing.

QUEER THINGS

"Very, very queer things have been happening to me
    In some of the places where I've been.
I went to the pillar-box this morning with a letter
    And a hand came out and took it in.

"When I got home again, I thought I'd have
    A glass of spirits to steady myself;
And I take my bible oath, but that bottle and glass
    Came a-hopping down off the shelf.

"No, no, I says, I'd better take no spirits,
    And I sat down to have a cup of tea;
And blowed if my old pair of carpet-slippers
    Didn't walk across the carpet to me!

"So I took my newspaper and went into the park,
    And looked round to see no one was near,
When a voice right out of the middle of the paper
    Started reading the news bold and clear!

"Well, I guess there's some magician out to help me,
    So perhaps there's no need for alarm;
And if I manage not to anger him,
    Why should he do me any harm?"

JAMES REEVES (1909–78)   237

MAGIC

Sandra's seen a leprechaun,
Eddie touched a troll,
Laurie danced with witches once,
Charlie found some goblins' gold.
Donald heard a mermaid sing,
Susy spied an elf,
But all the magic I have known
I've had to make myself.

ACKNOWLEDGMENTS

Thanks are due to the following copyright holders for permission to reprint:

HELEN ADAM: "Blue Moth, Black Magic" by Helen Adam, copyright © the Poetry Collection of the University Libraries, University at Buffalo, The State University of New York, and used with permission. FRANCISCO X. ALARCÓN: "Against Unruly Ants" from *Snake Poems*, University of Arizona Press, 1992. YEHUDA AMICHAI: "My Father" from *The Poetry of Yehuda Amichai*, Farrar, Straus & Giroux, 2015. A. R. AMMONS: "Appendix" from *Brink Road* by A. R. Ammons. Copyright © 1996 by A. R. Ammons. Used by permission of W. W. Norton & Company, Inc. SHUANG ANG: "The Magician's Daughter". Reprinted with permission from the poet. ANONYMOUS: "Charm for a Swarm of Bees," translated by David Barber. Copyright © 2011 by David Barber, from *The Word Exchange: Anglo-Saxon Poems in Translation*, edited by Greg Delanty and Michael Matto. Used by permission of W. W. Norton & Company, Inc. AMANDA AUCHTER: "The Magician's Girl" from *Bat City Review No. 2* (2006). CATHERINE BARNETT: "Chorus" from *The Game of Boxes*. Copyright © 2012 by Catherine Barnett. Reprinted with the permission of The Permissions Company, LLC on behalf of Graywolf Press, graywolfpress.org. NICKY BEER: "The Magicians at Work" from *Real Phonies and Genuine Fakes*. Copyright © 2023 by Nicky Beer. Reprinted with the permission of The Permissions Company, LLC on

241

behalf of Milkweed Editions, milkweed.org. MARGARET BENBOW: "Houdini Explodes from the Depths, Laughing." Reprinted with permission from the poet. ROWENA BASTIN BENNETT: "Thanksgiving Magic" originally published in *Child Life* magazine. Published by Rand McNally & Company, New York. RYAN BLACK: "The Conjurer," first published in *The Southern Review*. Reprinted with permission from the poet. MICHAEL BLUMENTHAL: "Sympathetic Magic" from *Sympathetic Magic*, Water Mark Press, 1980. JORGE LUIS BORGES: "Browning Resolves to Be a Poet" by Jorge Luis Borges, translated by Alastair Reid, copyright © 1999 by Maria Kodama; translation copyright © 1999 by Alastair Reid; from *Selected Poems* by Jorge Luis Borges, edited by Alexander Coleman. Used by permission of Viking Books, an imprint of Penguin Publishing Group, a division of Penguin Random House LLC. All rights reserved. MARILYN CHIN: "Cherry" (part of the *Fruit Études*) from *Poetry* (November 2020). Reprinted with permission from the poet. NICHOLAS CHRISTOPHER: "5° #21" from *5° and Other Poems*, Penguin Random House, Inc., 1995. Copyright © Nicholas Christopher. Reprinted with permission from Nicholas Christopher. SANDRA CISNEROS: "Night Madness Poem" from *Loose Woman* (Alfred A. Knopf, 1994). Stuart Bernstein Literary Agency. LUCILLE CLIFTON: "homage to my hips" copyright © 1980 by Lucille Clifton. Originally published by BOA Editions. Currently published in *good woman: poems and a memoir 1960–1980*. Reprinted by permission of Curtis Brown, Ltd. LEONARD COHEN: "Nothing I Can Lose" from *Flowers for Hitler* (McClelland and Stuart, 1964). Copyright